Upper Intermediate

Message Delivered

Paragraph Writing and Presentation

Leonid Yoffe
Soichiro Oku
Mari Kakuta
Yukinobu Satake
Akira Morita

NAN'UN-DO

Download Audio

音声ファイル
無料 DL
のご案内

このテキストの音声を無料で視聴（ストリーミング）・ダウンロードできます。自習用音声としてご活用ください。またモデル プレゼンテーションの映像も同ページにてご覧になれます。
以下のサイトにアクセスしてテキスト番号で検索してください。

https://nanun-do.com　テキスト番号［**512035**］

※ 無線 LAN（WiFi）に接続してのご利用を推奨いたします。

※ 音声ダウンロードは Zip ファイルでの提供になります。
お使いの機器によっては別途ソフトウェア（アプリケーション）の導入が必要となります。

Message Delivered <Upper Intermediate>

はしがき

本書 *Message Delivered <Upper Intermediate>* は、paragraph writing から presentation へとつなげることによって学習者の発信力を強化するレベル別英語教材のひとつとして作成されました。学習者の習熟度に応じて編纂された本シリーズの共通した主な意図と特徴は次の通りです。

1. Paragraph Writing の基礎、つまりその書式 (format) 、構造 (structure)、使うべき表現 (expressions) をきちんと身につける。
2. それらを的確に使いながら、英語の論理構成 (logic) と展開法 (organization) にのっとり的確に自分の考えを伝えることができる。
3. しっかりとした writing の基本を身に着けまとめられた自分の考え、意見を同じ論理構成を持った presentation の形として口頭で発表できる。
4. presentation の要点を、presenter として presentation を行うことによって学ぶだけでなく、より重要な audience の視点からの反省によって身につける。
5. これらに加えて、特に発信にとって重要な文法項目について整理を行う。

これらは英語の skill の面での学習の要点にもなるわけですが、それが本シリーズの最終的な目標ではありません。最終的な目標は、

a. 論理的な議論の展開（場合によっては日本語のそれとは違った）方法の基礎を知ること。
b. その論理の展開法を用いて物事を考え、自分の考えを、説得力を持って効率的に、そして正確に audience に伝えられ、同時にそうできるという自信を得ること。
c. 根拠を持った発言により、それを聞く人々 (audience) から信頼を得、グローバル人材の備えるべき発信面での能力向上を図る。

というものです。こうした目標を、本シリーズは学習者の習熟度に合わせたレベル別の構成によって、無理なく達成できるように企画されました。

その中で、本書 *Message Delivered <Upper Intermediate>* は、英語として表現、語彙のレベルを上げより自然に、また特に presentation では裏付けとなる資料等にも配慮しながら、内容的にも十分な説得力のある paragraph を書き presentation が行えるようタスクの求めるものに工夫をこらしています。これによって、paragraph からある程度の長さを持った essay へ、より信頼性のある presentation への発展は比較的容易なものであるはずです。そうした発展は、学習者の皆さんが、実際に何度も書き、発表することで体験しながら行ってください。それが著者一同の望みです。

なお、刊行にあたっては、株式会社南雲堂の加藤敦さんに企画段階から多くの助言をいただきました。加藤さんの忍耐力なくしては、本シリーズの完成はなかったでしょう。また、中原緑さんには、内容の点検も含め最終的な編集場面でご面倒をお掛けしました。この場を借りて御礼申し上げます。

著者一同

2019 年盛夏

本書の使い方

本書 *Message Delivered <Upper Intermediate>* では、到達目標として以下を掲げています。

1. Paragraph Writing の基礎を学び、ある程度の長さの paragraph を書けるようにすること。
2. paragraph を効果的な presentation として口頭発表ができること。
3. 読み手 (reader) や聞き手 (audience) を意識した paragraph を書き、presentation ができること。

本書の構成は次の通りです。

Part I（Unit 1-4） paragraph の書式 (format) 、構造 (structure) を学びます。
Part II（Unit 5-10） paragraph の論理構成 (logic)、展開法 (organization) を学びます。
Part III（Unit 11-14） presentation の要点と効果的な発表の仕方について学びます。

それぞれの Part には様々なタスクがありますが、それぞれの意図を参考に各自が予習・復習などの学習計画を組み立ててください。

Warm Up

各 Unit で扱うトピックに関する英語の知識を確認します。関連語句やトピックの概要を調べ、単語から文の形でまとめていきます。基本的な英文を書く力を見直すことも目標です。

Paragraph Analysis

各 Unit で扱う構造や論理構成、展開法について学びます。まず、Topic Sentence や Supporting Sentence などの用語の定義と実例を確認していきます。さらに Unit の重要項目の観点から Exercises A・B の model paragraph を分析して知識の定着を図ります。ここで用いられる表現や語句を使えるようにしていきましょう。また、論理構成や展開の仕方も model paragraph の中でどうなっているかを理解したうえで outline や writing の課題につなげていきますので、しっかりと学習内容を身に付けて書けるようにしてほしいところです。

Grammar for Writing

英文を書くときに注意しておきたい文法項目をまとめました。時制の使い分けや助動詞の意味、接続詞(特に従属接続詞と副詞節など)、形容詞と副詞などの基本的な項目を再確認し、実際に英文を書くときに参考にしてもらいたい内容です。空所補充や作文の形で理解度を測っていますが、まず参考書や辞書で該当する文法用語、例文は調べておくことが望ましいです。

Useful Vocabulary

Unit の中で用いられた語を英語による定義の中から選び、意味を確認する課題です。英英辞典を参照して英文の定義にあてはまる語を選択させる問題ですが、英英辞典をひくとどのような利点があるのか、オンラインの英英辞典などを参照して学んでもらいたいと思います。例文の中で英文の構造や文法項目にも注意してもらうようにしました。さらに、英和辞典の使い方、電子辞書と紙の辞書の使い分けや機能などを学びながら語彙学習の方略を確認しましょう。

Outline

これまで学んできたparagraphの構造や展開法を実際に書くための準備段階です。図表などに自分の考えていることを書いていく中で書く内容を整理していきます。語句レベルでのまとめから丁寧に学んできた文法項目などを使いながら一文、一文形にしていくプロセスを大事にしてください。

Writing

outlineでまとめた英文をparagraphの形に直していく課題です。英文の構造と内容の理解をもとに、特に主語、動詞、目的語、補語の形式と機能、修飾関係に注意を払って書く訓練をするとよいでしょう。

Your Own Presentation

Part IIIではUnit 10で書いたparagraphをpresentation用の原稿に書き換えていきます。presentationで用いる表現に気をつけ自分で実際に声を出しながら、またプレゼンテーション用のスライドを使いながら話す練習につなげていきます。また、相手に聞いてもらうように話すことと、人の発表を注意深く聞く練習も含まれていますので、学習者が相互に評価しながらすすめるとよいでしょう。

Contents

UNIT 1 Paragraphの構造

Formatting

学術的な文章を雑誌などに投稿する場合では、それぞれの投稿先によって決められた書式に従って文章を作成しなければなりません。本書では、以下の書式に沿ってparagraphの作成を行います。なお、以下の書式は、ワープロソフトで文章を作成することを前提にしていますが、手書きの場合もこれに準じて作成するようにしましょう。

title（タイトル）：最初の行にtitleを書く。できるだけ短いものの方が読み手に強い印象を与える。
　中央揃えにして、すべての単語の最初の文字を大文字にする。ただし、冠詞、前置詞、接続詞、代名詞などは、titleの先頭以外では小文字にする。

name and date（名前と日付）：ヘッダーに右寄せで名前と提出日を記入する。

indentation（インデント）：最初の文は3～5文字程度、右側に字下げをする。

line space（行間）：十分な行間を取る。目安は1行おきの行間。ワープロソフトの場合、行数を25行程度に設定する。

margin（余白）：上下左右に十分な余白を設定する。目安は、およそ以下の通り。
上 35mm
下 30mm
左右 35mm

alignment（配置）：「両端揃え」もしくは「左揃え」にする。

font（フォント）：CenturyやTimes New Romanが一般的。本文の文字サイズは12ポイント程度の見やすいサイズにする。titleは本文よりも少し大きなサイズにする。

line break（改行）：語の途中での改行はできるだけ避ける。また、1つの文ごとに改行するようなことはしない。

paper（用紙）：A4用紙

Takashi Yamamoto
April 13, 20XX

The Best Country for Me

　There are three reasons why Canada is one of the best countries in the world. First, Canada has an excellent health care system. All Canadians have access to medical services at a reasonable price. Second, Canada has a high standard of education. Students are taught by well-trained teachers and are encouraged to continue studying at university. Finally, Canada's cities are clean and efficiently managed. Canadian cities have many parks and lots of space for people to live. As a result, Canada is a desirable place to live.

Exercise A

以下の 2 つの paragraph について、書式上の問題点を指摘しましょう。

(a)

Takashi Yamamoto
April 13, 20XX

My favorite season

Fall is definitely my favorite season of the year. First, it is the most beautiful of the four seasons. The leaves of the trees seem to explode into glorious colors: red, orange, gold, and brown. Next, the temperature in the fall is perfect. The days in the low twenties are neither too hot nor uncomfortably chilly, and the nighttime temperatures make for a great night's sleep. Finally, my favorite holiday of the year, Thanksgiving, is in the fall. Most of the people get a few days off in October or November to spend time with friends and family while enjoying delicious food. More than any other season, the fall is my favorite time of year.

(b)

My Favorite Season

Fall is definitely my favorite season of the year. First, it is the most beautiful of the four seasons.
The leaves of the trees seem to explode into glorious colors: red, orange, gold, and brown.
Next, the temperature in the fall is perfect.
The days in the low twenties are neither too hot nor uncomfortably chilly, and the nighttime temperatures make for a great night's sleep.
Finally, my favorite holiday of the year, Thanksgiving, is in the fall.
Most of the people get a few days off in October or November to spend time with friends and family while enjoying delicious food.
More than any other season, the fall is my favorite time of year.

Paragraph Structure

一つの話題について述べているいくつかの文のかたまりのことをParagraphと言います。paragraphは、以下の構成要素が順序良く並べられることによって読者に伝わりやすくなります。

☆ Topic Sentence（主題文）: paragraphの話題とその話題に対する筆者の考えを提示する文で、通常paragraphの先頭に置かれます。

☆ Supporting Sentences（支持文）: topic sentenceで提示した考えがいかに正しいのかを、具体例や理由などを示して、裏付ける文です。具体例や理由などの数に応じて、複数の支持文を置くことになります。

▷ Details（ディテールズ）: supporting sentencesに続いて、支持文の補足をする文です。それぞれの支持文に1～2文を加えるのが普通です。

☆ Concluding Sentence（まとめ文）: supporting sentencesの内容をまとめたり、topic sentenceの主張を別のことばで言い換えたりしてparagraph全体をまとめる文のことです。通常は、パラグラフの最後に置かれます。

＊ 本書では、topic sentence（1文）+ supporting sentences（3文）+ details（3文）+ concluding sentence（1文）の8文からなるparagraphを書く練習をしていきます。

2

Takashi Yamamoto
April 13, 20XX

The Best Country for Me

There are three reasons why Canada is one of the best
Topic Sentence
countries in the world. First, Canada has an excellent health
Supporting Sentence 1
care system. All Canadians have access to medical services
Detail 1
at a reasonable price. Second, Canada has a high standard
Supporting Sentence 2
of education. Students are taught by well-trained teachers
Detail 2
and are encouraged to continue studying at university.
Finally, Canada's cities are clean and efficiently managed.
Supporting Sentence 3
Canadian cities have many parks and lots of space for people
Detail 3
to live. As a result, Canada is a desirable place to live.
Concluding Sentence

3つのsupporting sentencesを、文頭のtopic sentence、文末のconcluding sentenceで挟み込むような形にします。

3つのsupporting sentencesには、それぞれ一つのdetailを付けます。

合計8つの文で一つのparagraphを完成させます。

Exercise B

次の paragraph を読み、以下の質問に答えましょう。

My Hobby

(1) Listening to music is one of my favorite hobbies. (2) Listening to various kinds of music allows me to become more familiar with cultures from around the world, something I enjoy very much. (3) I can listen to Japanese music, Western music, African music and many genres of music online. (4) The second reason why I like to listen to music is it calms me down. (5) I love to listen to music when I commute to school because it is relaxing. (6) Being able to talk to friends about my favorite musicians is another reason why I enjoy this hobby. (7) I like to exchange new information about different musicians with my friends. (8) These are just a few of the reasons why I enjoy listening to music.

1. Topic sentence を番号で指摘し、その内容を日本語で説明しましょう。

Topic sentence (　　)　　内容：

2. Supporting sentences とそれぞれの supporting sentences に続く detail を番号で指摘し、その内容を日本語で説明しましょう。

Supporting sentence 1 (　　) 内容：

Detail (　　)　　内容：

Supporting sentence 2 (　　) 内容：

Detail (　　)　　内容：

Supporting sentence 3 (　　) 内容：

Detail (　　)　　内容：

3. Concluding sentence の文を番号で指摘し、どのようなまとめ方をしているのかを日本語で説明しましょう。

Concluding sentence (　　)　まとめ方：

Exercise C

次の paragraph の空欄に入る文を下から選び、paragraph を完成させましょう。 4

My Hobby

Baking is one of my favorite hobbies. ____________________________________ __________. I can choose to follow the recipe exactly as written, or I can change the recipe by adding new ingredients. ____________________________________ ________. I love to go to the grocery store to shop for ingredients, and then combine them all together to make a product that many people enjoy. __________ ____________________________________. Many of my friends look forward to the tasty treats that I share with them. ____________________________________ ____.

(1) Baking allows me to be creative, which I enjoy.

(2) These are just a few of the reasons why I enjoy baking.

(3) Being able to share things that I bake is another reason why I enjoy this hobby.

(4) The second reason why I like to bake is because the entire process of baking is fun for me.

Grammar for Writing

文の構造

文の構造の 3 タイプ
英語の文には 3 つのタイプがあります。

1. 単文：S + V の関係が一つだけで、主節のみで成り立っている文
   I like coffee.
   The earth goes around the sun.
   Mary did not go to the party.

2. 重文：2 つ以上の節が等位接続詞やセミコロンで結ばれた文
   I like coffee and Mary likes tea.
   Mary went to work but no one was there.
   Our car broke down; we came last.

3. 複文：主節の他に従属節を含む文
   We missed our plane because we were late.
   Our dog barks when she hears a noise.
   Do you know the man who is talking to Mary?

Exercise D

次の文がどのタイプの文であるか、分類しましょう（単文、重文、複文)。

1. John did not enjoy the school festival.

2. I went to school but the class was canceled.

3. John gets upset when he has to go to his English class.

4. John is a teacher and Jane is a student.

5. I like eating chocolates.

Exercise E

日本語を参考に与えられた語を並び替えましょう。(文頭に来る語も小文字で始めています。)

1. 彼は、テニスをするのが好きです。
   (likes / playing / he / tennis).

2. 雨が降っていますが、試合は行います。
   (match / it / raining / is / we / hold / but / will / the).

3. 彼女は、英語が得意ですが、彼は苦手です。
   (isn’t / but / at / is / she / good / English / he).

4. ジェーンは、お菓子がある時にしか来ません。
   (snacks / provide / when / Jane / only / comes / they).

UNIT 2 Topic Sentence

Paragraph を構成する最も重要な文は topic sentence です。この文章を読むことによって、paragraph の内容がつかめなくてはなりません。よい topic sentence を書くことで、よい paragraph を書くことができます。この unit では以下の点を到達目標とします：

- Topic sentence のテーマの絞り方を学ぶ。
- Topic sentence の構成、書き方を学ぶ。
- Simple present（現在形）について学習し、理解する。

Warm Up

A. アメリカについて調べて、どのような特徴があるか、以下のポイントを中心に英語で箇条書きで書きましょう。

People (人), Food (食べ物), Customs (慣習)

People
・(Ex.) American people tend to be friendly
・
・
Food
・(Ex.) American cuisine has had a lot of influence from Mexico.
・
・
Customs
・(Ex.) American people celebrate Independence Day on July 4th.
・
・

B. 自分があげたアメリカの特徴について互いに紹介し、意見を交換し合いましょう。

Paragraph Analysis

Paragraph の基本的な構成は、paragraph の背景や情報を伝える introductory sentence（導入文）, paragraph の一番言いたいことを提示する topic sentence（主題文）, topic sentence で提示されたことを裏付けする supporting sentences（支持文）, supporting sentences に続いて、その内容を補足する details（ディテールズ）と最後に supporting sentences をまとめたり、topic sentence を別の言葉で言い換える concluding sentence（まとめの文）よりなっています。

Topic sentence は、introductory sentences に続き paragraph の前半に来ることが多く、paragraph で一番書き手が言いたいことが書かれています。

Topic sentence とは、main idea（主題）となる topic と assertion（主張）, limitation（制限）または condition（条件）を 1 文に書いたものです。

Understanding different cultures is an important skill that a teacher must have.

Understanding different cultures	is an important skill	that a teacher must have.
topic	assertion	limitation

< Useful Expressions >

Topic sentence の main idea を書くときに意見を主張する言い回しを復習しましょう。

It can be said ...

It can be said that Japanese people tend to be quiet compared to Americans.

A can be B ...

For Japanese people, stating their opinion directly can be a difficult task.

Exercise A

次の paragraph を読み、以下の質問に答えましょう。 5

For many North Americans doing business in Japan can be a very challenging experience. This is due, in part, to the way people make decisions in each culture. Generally speaking, the Japanese prefer to discuss matters in a group and reach an agreement collectively. On the other hand, in the West people are more prepared to act individually. The roots of this phenomenon are historic and go back hundreds of years. In Western societies, personal drive, ambition and risk-taking are valued, while Japanese culture emphasizes one's ability to work with others and the contribution a person can make to a team. Both approaches have their respective benefits and drawbacks. For example, a benefit of the Japanese tradition to work as a group is that all members of a team have an opportunity to voice their opinion. However, building a consensus requires a long time and it is not easy to reach a decision quickly.

1. 上の paragraph の main idea は何ですか？
2. Topic sentence に線を引きましょう。
3. "For many North Americans doing business in Japan can be a very challenging experience" この理由を書きましょう。

Exercise B

以下の topic sentence を読み、1つ選びましょう。なぜそれを選んだのか、どのような内容で paragraph を書くことができるか、ペアで話し合いましょう。

1. Japanese people tend to be quiet compared to Americans.
2. To communicate well across cultures we must have mutual respect.
3. Japanese food contains many ingredients that are good for a healthy diet.
4. There are many traditional celebrations in Japan that are based on different religions.
5. North Americans doing business in Japan may face a number of cultural problems.

[　　　]
選んだ理由：
paragraph の内容：

Grammar for Writing

Simple Present

Simple Present（現在形）は、通常は、動詞の原形を用います。３人称単数が主語の時には、動詞の原形の語尾に -e(s) を付けます。普通は、原形に -s を付けますが（jump → jumps）、s, z, sh, ch などの音の後には、-es をつけます（brush → brushes）。

Simple Present（現在形）は、以下の時に使用します。

1. 現在の状況や、習慣的、繰り返し行う動作
   She lives in a big house.（彼女は大きな家に住んでます。）
   He eats bread every morning.（彼は毎朝パンを食べます。）
   Mr. Johnson teaches history.（ジョンソンさんは歴史を教えています。）

2. 不変の事実
   The sun rises in the east.（日は、東から昇ります。）

Exercise C

日本語を参考に（　　　）に適切な英語を入れましょう。

1. 父は毎朝、家の近くの公園で走ります。
   My father (　　　　　　) in the park near our house every day.

2. 母は、毎週 , カーテンを洗います。
   My mother (　　　　　　) the curtains every week.

3. 日本人は、1 月の初めに幸運を祈りに（初詣）に行きます。
   Japanese people (　　　　　　) to pray for good fortune (*hatsumoude*) at the beginning of January.

4. アメリカ人は、独立記念日を 7 月 4 日にお祝いします。
   Americans (　　　　　　) Independence Day on the 4th of July.

Exercise D

次の topic sentence について、日本語を参考に与えられた語を並び替えましょう。（文頭に来る語も小文字で始めています。）

1. Doing business in America can be (for / Japanese / due / to / cultural / difficult / differences / several).
   アメリカでビジネスをすることは、日本人にとって、様々な文化の違いによって難しいです。

2. Japanese food for the New Year (meanings / have / uses / ingredients / that / many / many).
   お正月の食べ物は、様々な食材を使いそれらは意味を持っています。

3. Japanese manga culture (is / because / overseas / of / the / following / popular / reasons).
   日本の漫画カルチャーは以下の理由により海外でとても人気です。

4. (many / their / use / that / English / first / language / countries / as) has different vocabulary for words that reflect their culture and customs.
   英語を第一言語とする国々では、その国の文化や慣習を反映している用語などがあります。

Useful Vocabulary

Exercise E

次の語の定義を a. から j. の中から選んで、記号で答えましょう。

____ 1. cultivate
____ 2. misunderstanding
____ 3. tradition
____ 4. prevalent
____ 5. comparison
____ 6. perspective
____ 7. accommodate
____ 8. adopt
____ 9. frustration
____ 10. hesitate

a. a belief or ways that a particular group of people have continued or inherited
b. an examination of two or more items to establish similarities and dissimilarities
c. to adapt to something
d. to be reluctant
e. to choose or use
f. views or ways of thinking
g. to grow or nurture
h. to feel distress or to be annoyed with something
i. failure to understand something correctly
j. existing very commonly

Outline

Title を考えましょう

Topic sentence では、書き手が一番いいたいことが書かれているので、topic sentence を要約すると title になります。ただ、title は読み手の興味をひかなくてはならないので、工夫が必要です。以下の topic sentence の title を考えてみましょう。

Japanese people tend to be less direct and not so assertive compared to Americans.

ヒント：質問形式にしたり、インパクトがあるキーワードを使ってみてください。

Listing

上の title を参考に、paragraph を書くときに書けそうな項目を箇条書きしてみましょう。

Title:

・

・

・

・

・

Writing

上の Outline をもとに、日本とアメリカの文化の違いについて一つの paragraph にまとめてみましょう。

UNIT 3 Supporting Sentences

Unit 2 で学んだ、topic sentence の後には、 3 ～ 4 の supporting sentences を書かなければなりません。supporting sentences は topic sentence で書かれている、内容（主題）について、具体例や理由など述べて、topic sentence で言いたいことを強化する役割を持っています。よい supporting sentences を書くことによってより内容のある段落を書くことができます。この unit では以下の点を到達目標とします：

- Supporting sentences の書き方を学ぶ。
- Supporting sentences の書く順番について学ぶ。
- Simple past（過去形）について学習し、理解する。

Warm Up

A. 自分が好きな科目を 2 つ選び、なぜその科目が好きなのか、理由をリストにしましょう。

(Ex). English
・(Ex.) I can communicate with many people from all over the world. ・(Ex.) I like the way my English teacher teaches. ・(Ex.) Learning about language rules is very interesting.
・ ・ ・
・ ・ ・

B. 自分があげた授業について、ペアでお互い書いたことをシェアしましょう。

Paragraph Analysis

Supporting sentencesとは、topic sentenceで書いた内容を、サポートし、補強する役割を持っています。基本的には、topic sentenceの後に、3つのsupporting sentencesが書かれることが多いようです。supporting sentencesでは、topic sentenceの主張を強化するために、理由、事実、具体例などを述べます。

< Useful Expressions >

Supporting sentencesは理由、事実、具体例などを、順番に並べて、書かなくてはいけません。そのため、3つのsupporting sentencesを書く時にtransition（文の転換）が重要となってきます。

1. first, second, third など数字を使うもの。
2. next など、次の内容を表すもの。
3. however, on the other hand, in contrast to など内容の対比や比較などができるもの。

Exercise A

次の paragraph を読み、以下の質問に答えましょう。

The name itself comes from ancient Greece where the first Games were held in a place called Olympia. A thousand five hundred years later the Olympics returned and the first modern Olympic Games took place in Athens in 1896. Only men participated at that time. Since then, the Summer and Winter Olympic Games have been organized regularly, every four years, except during World War I and World War II. We tend to think of the Olympic Games as a sporting event; however, it was not always the case. In fact, between 1912 and 1948, artists, painters and musicians all competed for medals in their respective fields. Today, the Olympic Games are a huge celebration lasting two weeks. For example, the most recent Summer games in Rio de Janeiro in 2016 attracted more than 10,000 athletes from over 200 countries.

1. この文章は、Olympic について書かれていますが、Olympic について書かれている情報を３つリストにしましょう。

   ・
   ・
   ・

2. この段落に、適した topic sentence を書きましょう。

Exercise B

以下の topic sentence を読んで、3 つの supporting sentences を選び、その選んだ理由を書きましょう。また、選ばなかった文についても、なぜ選ばなかったのか理由を書きましょう。

Topic Sentence

English education in Japan has changed over the years to enhance Japanese students' communication skills.

1. Japanese tend to translate English directly to Japanese.

2. First, English teachers in Japan used a grammar-translation method which made students understand grammar.

3. English has many varieties and is spoken all over the world.

4. The grammar-translation method was very effective and many students could read and write but had weak in communication skills.

5. Now, the communicative approach is used in many schools in Japan to improve students' ability to interact with others.

[　　] [　　] [　　]
選んだ理由：
[　　] [　　]
選ばなかった理由：

Grammar for Writing

Simple Past

Simple Past（過去形）は、規則変化動詞では、人称に関係なく動詞の原形の語尾に -ed, -d を付けます。不規則変化動詞は、活用形が異なるので、よく復習しましょう（make, run, sit, go, be, etc.）。動詞の原形と過去形の形が変わらないものもあります。（cost, cut, spread, etc.）

Simple Past（過去形）は、以下の時に使用する

1. 過去の動作や出来事
   Jane was an outgoing child in kindergarten but now she is very shy.（ジェーンは、活発な子供でしたが、今はとても恥ずかしがり屋です。）
   Tokyo Olympics ended successfully in 1964.（東京オリンピックは 1964 年に成功して終わりました。）

2. 過去の習慣的な動作や、繰り返し行っていた動作、長期間の状態
   I often went to my grandmother's house when I was small.（私は小さい時よく、祖母の家に行きました。）
   In those days, the city was crowded with people wanting to see the cherry blossoms.（当時、街は、桜を見たい人で、混雑していました。）
   This school was once a hospital during the war.（この学校は以前、戦争中の時には病院でした。）

Exercise C

日本語を参考に（　　　）に適切な英語を入れましょう。

1. 彼女は、昨日パーティ用のサンドイッチを作りました。
   Yesterday, she (　　　　　　) sandwiches for the party.
2. 昨年の夏には、この店は、かき氷を買う客でいっぱいでした。
   Last summer, this shop (　　　　　　) crowded with people buying shaved ice.
3. 私は、小学生の時によく、従兄弟と遊びました。
   When I was in elementary school, I often (　　　　　　) with my cousin.
4. 江戸時代では、人々は着物を着ていました。
   During the Edo period people (　　　　　　) kimonos.

Exercise D

日本語を参考に与えられた語句を並び替えましょう。（文頭に来る語も小文字で始めています。）

1. When I was six years old (elementary / near / I / my / entered / school / house / an).
   6歳の時に、家の近くの小学校に入学しました。

   ....

2. (for / hard / students / studied / the national exam / many).
   多くの学生は、国家試験のために勉強しました。

   ....

3. English was taught only from junior high school (taught / but / it / is / from / elementary / now / school).
   英語は、中学校から教えられていましたが、今は、小学校から教えられています。

   ....

Useful Vocabulary

Exercise E

次の語の定義を a. から j. の中から選んで、記号で答えましょう。

____ 1. compulsory
____ 2. continue
____ 3. national
____ 4. satisfaction
____ 5. evaluate
____ 6. outcomes
____ 7. quantitative
____ 8. memorize
____ 9. apply
____ 10. standard

a. to keep going
b. accepted as normal
c. countrywide
d. to learn by heart
e. test, judge
f. results
g. fulfillment; contentment
h. describing the amount of something rather than how good it is
i. to use
j. required

Outline

Warm up をもとに、自分が好きな科目について、なぜ好きなのか、そして何の役に立つか、将来の夢と絡めて書いてみましょう。ここでは、順序を気にしながら、好きになったきっかけ、その科目が自分にとって何の役に立つのか、そして将来どのように応用できるのか、内容を整理して書いてみましょう。

Why I came to like the subject
Why the subject is important to me
How I can apply the knowledge and experience in my future work

Writing

上のをもとに、好きな科目について一つの paragraph にまとめてみましょう。

UNIT 4 Concluding Sentence

Concluding sentence とは paragraph の最後に書く文のことで、paragraph 全体をまとめる役割を持っています。concluding sentence では、topic sentence の main idea や、supporting sentences で topic を support した内容を 1 文程度でまとめなくてはなりません。concluding sentence を書くことによって、paragraph の構成が完成します。この unit では以下の点を到達目標とします：

- Concluding sentence の書き方を学ぶ。
- Paragraph structure (構成) のおさらいをする。
- Present Perfect（現在完了）について学習し、理解する。

Warm Up

A. 世界の言語の中で、興味がある言語を 2 つ選んで、その言語について以下の項目を調べて、まとめてみましょう。

History/Characteristics
Countries or places where it is used/Number of speakers
Regional variations/dialects

B. 自分が選んだ言語について、ペアでお互い書いたことをシェアしましょう。

Paragraph Analysis

Concluding sentence とは、topic sentence で書いた内容を言い換え、supporting sentences によって強化された内容をまとめる役割を持っています。基本的には、paragraph の最後に書かれることが多いようです。concluding sentence では、作者の言いたいメッセージが、topic sentence のまとめたものに付け足されていることが多いです。

< Useful Expressions >

Concluding sentence を書くときに以下の書き出しが、便利です。

1. **To summarize, summing up, in short, in brief, to wrap up** のような「まとめると」という意味合いを持っているフレーズ。

2. **In conclusion, as a result, concluding the essay** など「最後に、最後にまとめると」という意味を持っているフレーズ。

Exercise A

次の paragraph を読み、以下の質問に答えましょう。

Sign language is not really one language but a variety of languages which have evolved across the world over hundreds of years. As a result of this complicated history, today we have 35 sign languages in North and South America. People have used American Sign Language for well over 200 years, and it is considered to be one of the oldest established sign languages in the world.

Sign languages typically use not only gestures but also facial expressions. Both depend on the country where the sign language is used. Thus, for example, in the United States speakers use only one hand when fingerspelling while in Britain and in Germany both hands are used. A study of a sign language can open the door to a fascinating world — you would be amazed to discover how it can help convey every nuance of human thought and emotion!

1. 上の paragraph の main idea は何ですか？

2. Topic sentence に線を引きましょう。

3. 作者が伝えたかったことは何でしょうか？本文に線を引き、和訳しましょう。

Exercise B

以下の文を正しい順番に並べ替え、[　　]にその番号を書き、その後に続く concluding sentence を書いてみましょう。

[　　] Now many people study sign language and even in elementary schools many children are taught how to sign in the assembly or extra-curricular activities.

[　　] Also, sign language has become popular thanks to TV dramas that feature Deaf main characters.

[　　] Deaf people have been regarded as inferior to hearing people but now gradually, people's views towards the Deaf are changing.

[　　] First, Deaf people are regarded as a linguistic minority who use sign language as their first language.

(注：d を大文字の D に変え Deaf と使う事によって、日本手話を母語とするろう者を表している。日本人を Japanese と表わすのと同様に大文字を使用します)

Concluding sentence

(　　　　　　　　　　　　　　　　　　　　　　　　　　　　　　　　　　　)

Grammar for Writing

Present Perfect

Present Perfect（現在完了）は、過去に起こった動作や状態を現在に結びつけるときに使用され、have[has]+ 過去分詞で用いられます。

Present Perfect（現在完了）は、以下の時に使用します。

1. 現在までにし終えた行為（完了）
   I have just finished writing my essay.（今宿題をし終えたところです。）
   She has just eaten that big doughnut.（彼女は大きなドーナツを食べ終えたところでした。）

2. 過去にしたこと（経験）
   I have visited New York three times.（3 回ニューヨークを訪れたことがあります。）
   She has been to Jane's house several times.（数回ジェーンの家に遊びに行ったことがあります。）

3. 今現在の状況が過去にしたことの結果によって成り立っているとき（結果）
   I have eaten my breakfast.（朝ごはんを食べてしまいました。）
   I have lost my keys.（鍵をなくしてしまいました。）

4. 過去から現在まで継続的に続いていることを表すとき（継続）
   I have lived in Tokyo for 5 years.（東京に 5 年住んでいます。）
   Tim has played tennis for 3 years.（ティムはテニスを 3 年やっています。）

Exercise C

Grammar for writing の例文を参考に、日本語を英語に直しましょう。

1. 私は、夕食を食べてしまいました。

2. 私たちは、京都に 5 年住んでいます。

3. 彼らは、6 回日本を訪れたことがあります。

4. ジョンは、ノートをなくしてしまいました。

Exercise D

次の concluding sentence の空欄に、適切な英語を書きましょう。

1. I ( ) ( ) football for two years and it is the most interesting sport I have ever played.

2. I ( ) ( ) to New York 4 times and am fascinated by its diverse culture.

3. I ( ) ( ) my motivation to study but learning a new language allowed me to make a lot of new friends.

4. The native people of the country ( ) ( ) their heritage due to colonization.

Useful Vocabulary

Exercise E

次の語の定義を a. から j. の中から選んで、記号で答えましょう。

_____ 1. diversity
_____ 2. origin
_____ 3. natives
_____ 4. first language
_____ 5. dialect
_____ 6. cultural conflict
_____ 7. language contact
_____ 8. language imperialism
_____ 9. minority
_____ 10. majority

a. a particular form of a language which is peculiar to a specific region or social group
b. mother tongue
c. a dispute between people from different backgrounds
d. when a language has more power over other languages
e. the smaller number
f. the social and linguistic phenomenon which occurs when speakers of different languages interact with one another
g. the greater number
h. the original people living in a specific area
i. where something begins
j. a range of different things or people

Outline

Warm up をもとに、ある言語について、そしてその歴史、使っている人たちや文化などの要素をいれた paragraph を書くために、outline を書いてみましょう。outline では、supporting sentences に入れる内容を英語や日本語で箇条書きし、paragraph structure を工夫してみましょう。

I. Introduction
II.
III.
IV.
V. Conclusion

Writing

前の outline をもとに、選んだ言語について一つの paragraph に書いてみましょう。

UNIT 5

AIの長所・短所について書いてみよう（Listing）

Part II

ある物事を説明する際に、その長所や短所を列挙すると分かりやすくなることがあります。この unit では以下の点を目標とします。

・ Listing の paragraph の構造を理解し、よく使われる表現・語彙を学ぶ。
・ Listing の paragraph の outline を作成し、完成する。
・ Present progressive（現在進行形）について学習し、理解する。

Warm Up

A. AI（artificial intelligence ＝人工知能）がもたらす良い点（benefits）と悪い点（drawbacks）について自分なりに考え、下の表に書きこんでみましょう。

Benefits
・ (Ex.) People don’t have to perform boring or dangerous tasks anymore.
・
・
・
・
Drawbacks
・ (Ex.) AI may come to control human beings.
・
・
・
・

B. 自分が挙げた AI の benefits と drawbacks について互いに紹介し、意見を交換し合いましょう。

Paragraph Analysis

Listing タイプの paragraph とは、様々な事柄や例などを挙げていく paragraph です。例えば何かの良い点や悪い点、何か事を行うにあたって気をつけなくてはならない点、何かを調査した結果分かったことを列挙する際などに、このタイプの paragraph がよく用いられます。

< Useful Expressions >

このタイプの **paragraph** で用いられる表現には以下のようなものがあります：

first, second, third, another（別の）, first of all, lastly, finally, last of all（最後に）, most importantly（最も重要なものとして）, last but not least（最後に述べるが決して軽んずべきでないものとして）, some ... others ～（…という者もいれば～という者もいる）

Exercise A

次の paragraph を読み、以下の質問に答えましょう。

Modern technology depends more and more on artificial intelligence (AI) to perform its functions. As science advances, artificial intelligence is expected to play an increasingly prominent role in our society. While there are a number of exciting benefits, we should not forget about potential risks. (①　　　　　　　), as companies are relying more on machines, many jobs will be lost. We are beginning to see this trend in many industries already. (②　　　　　　　), we are likely to forget many skills because they simply won't be required in the future. Perhaps most (③　　　　　　　) many experts are asking the question: "As the power of machines grows, will the moment come when they will control us instead of us controlling them?"

1. 上の paragraph の main idea は何ですか？

2. Useful Expressions を参考に、上の中の（　）に適切な語(句）を入れましょう。

3. 上の paragraph で述べている AI がもたらす risk について全て挙げてみましょう。

・

・

・

・

Exercise B

次の paragraph を読み、以下の質問に答えましょう。

Every day we are seeing many very fluent English speakers around us. Did you ever wonder what makes them successful in their study? I believe the secret is their level of motivation. Many factors have an impact on our motivation to become more proficient in English. (①) enjoy communication with people from other cultures. They are always looking for opportunities to travel overseas and learn something new. (②) want to understand English songs, movies and literature better. Knowledge of English allows them to expand their horizons. (③), many of us are influenced by our teachers. After all, role models are very important. If we are inspired, most of us will want to make an extra effort. What do you think motivates you?

1. 上の paragraph の main idea は何ですか？

2. Useful Expressions を参考に、上の paragraph 中の（　）に適切な語を入れましょう。

3. 上の paragraph で述べられている英語学習の動機づけの理由を全て見つけ、下の表を完成させましょう。また、それぞれの理由を補強する上で、どんなことが書かれていますか？

Reasons to study English	Support for each reason
First reason:	
Second reason:	
Third reason:	

Grammar for Writing

Present Progressive

Present Progressive（現在進行形）は、現在時制が永続的・習慣的行為を表すのに対し、一時的な行為などを表します（Ex. Businesses are relying on complex robots more and more.）。他に以下のような用法があります。

1. 確定された近い未来の予定
   I am leaving for New York on a business trip.（←確定された予定）
   cf. I will leave for New York on a business trip.（←その場で決めた未来の意志）

2. 現在の反復的動作（always などを伴い、不快・苛立ちなどの感情を表します）
   He is always annoying me with his rude jokes.（彼はいつも失礼な冗談で私をいらいらさせる。）

3. 動作の完結に近づいている状態
   Many minor languages are dying.（多くの少数言語は死にかけています。）

Exercise C

日本語を参考に（　　　）に適切な英語を入れましょう。

1. あの木の下で何かが動いています。
   Something (　　　　　　) under that tree.

2. その電車は今止まりかけています。
   The train (　　　　　　) now.

3. トムはいつも会議に遅れてばかりいます。
   Tom (　　　　　　) late to the meeting.

4. 私は来週田舎に帰る予定です。
   I (　　　　　　) back home next week.

Exercise D

日本語を参考に、現在進行形を使って ……… の部分を英語に直しましょう。必要に応じてモデルパラグラフも参考にすること。

1. 現在、多くの企業が再生可能（renewable）エネルギーに依存しています。

   Now many companies ....

2. ジムはいつもいらいらさせる質問ばかりします。

   Jim ....

3. 多くのヨーロッパの国々は原子力（nuclear）エネルギーの使用を禁止しつつあります。

   A number of European countries ....

4. 彼女はいつも英語を話す機会を探しています。

   She ....

5. 私は有名なオクトーバーフェスト（Octoberfest）に出席するために来週ドイツに行く予定です。

   I ....

Part II

Useful Vocabulary

Exercise E

次の語の定義を a. から j. の中から選んで、記号で答えましょう。

_____	1. prominent	a.	one of several things that influence or cause something
_____	2. potential	b.	to encourage someone by making them feel confident and eager to do something
_____	3. overlook	c.	to make something greater in size, number or importance
_____	4. proficient	d.	to fail to see or notice something
_____	5. factor	e.	created by people; not happening naturally
_____	6. literature	f.	important; famous
_____	7. expand	g.	pieces of writing that are valued as works of art
_____	8. horizon	h.	competent or skilled in doing or using something
_____	9. artificial	i.	likely to develop into something in the future
_____	10. inspire	j.	the limit of a person's knowledge, experience, or interest

Outline

最近読んで印象に残っている新聞記事やインターネット上のニュースを取り上げ、なぜそれが印象に残っているか、その理由をいくつか下の表に書き出してみましょう。

An article which left an impression on you
The key points of this article
・ ・ ・ ・ ・ ・ ・ ・ ・ ・ ・ ・ ・

Writing

上の outline をもとに、その記事やニュースがなぜ印象に残っているかを説明する paragraph を書いてみましょう。

UNIT 6 人の伝記を書いてみよう（Chronological Order）

人の伝記などを書く場合は、物事を起こった順に書いていきます。この unit では以下の点を目標とします。

・ Chronological order の paragraph の構造を理解し、よく使われる表現・語彙を学ぶ。
・ Chronological order の paragraph の outline を作成し、完成する。
・ Modal（will, must, have to）について学習し、理解する。

Warm Up

A. 他のクラスメイトのこれまでの人生について聞きたい質問を考え（When were you born?, Where were you born?, etc.)、それを互いに質問し合い、メモを取ってみましょう。

Question: ....

Answer: ....

Question: ....

Answer: ....

Question: ....

Answer: ....

B. 上のメモにもとづいて、そのクラスメイトの人生を他のクラスメイトに英語で簡単に紹介してみましょう。

Paragraph Analysis

Chronological Order Paragraph とは、出来事を起こった順に説明していく paragraph です。例えば物語や歴史的出来事、有名人の伝記などを書く際に、このタイプの paragraph を使います。また、何かのプロセスや手順を説明する際にもこのタイプの paragraph がよく用いられます。例えば写真の撮り方、科学の実験の仕方、口座を開く方法などです。

＜Useful Expressions＞

時や理由、条件を表す副詞節を導く接続表現には次のようなものがあります：

before（の前に）, after（の後に）, while（一方で）, until（まで）, as soon as（するやいなや）, when（の時）, because, since, as（～なので）, if（もし）

時間的な順序を表す副詞（句）には次のようなものがあります：

now, then, first, second, next, soon, later, gradually, eventually, finally, at the same time, meanwhile（そうこうするうちに）

Exercise A

次の paragraph を読み、以下の質問に答えましょう。

Steve Jobs was one of the greatest entrepreneurs and innovators of our time. He was born in 1955 in San Francisco. At age 13, he had a summer job at Hewlett-Packard Company and became interested in electronics. In 1972, Jobs entered Reed College in Portland, USA, but dropped out the same year. In 1976, he and Steven Wozniak co-founded Apple Inc. In 1985, he was forced out from the company because many senior managers couldn't understand his vision. He founded a successful company which eventually became a part of Apple. Then, in 1997 he returned to his former company and became CEO in 1997. In the later 1990s, business at Apple was not good; however, the company launched a string of revolutionary products such as the iPod, iPhone and iPad. Steve Jobs had a unique ability to understand what the needs of the people would be five or ten years later and create technology to meet those needs.

1. 上の paragraph の main idea は何ですか？

2. 上の paragraph で述べられている出来事の前後関係を理解する助けとなっている言葉は何だと思いますか？

3. 上の paragraph の趣旨に沿って、下の表を完成させましょう。最初の空欄は埋めてあります。

year	What happened?
In 1955	Jobs was born in San Francisco.

Exercise B

次の paragraph を読み、以下の質問に答えましょう。 11

It is easy to order books online. Now, many companies ship books to Japan from overseas. (①) you should decide which company you would like to use. (②) go to that company's homepage. The (③) step is to type the name of the author or the title of the book to check if it is available. If the book is in stock you will need to provide information for delivery and payment, such as your address and your credit card number. You will also need to specify how the book should be shipped. Fast delivery is always more expensive. There you have it! It will (④) arrive in your mailbox.

1. 上の paragraph の main idea は何ですか？
2. Useful Expressions を参考に、上の paragraph 中の（ ）に適切な語を入れてみましょう。
3. 上の paragraph の趣旨に沿って、下の表を完成させましょう。

インターネットで本を注文するには、

まず、
次に、
その後、
最後に、

Grammar for Writing

Modals 1 (will, must, have to)

Modal（助動詞）は、話し手の判断などの心的態度を示す品詞で、動詞の原形が続きます。have to を除き、疑問文では助動詞が文頭に、否定文では助動詞の後に not をつけ、その後に動詞の原形が来ます。

We'll go shopping tomorrow.（肯定）
Will we go shopping tomorrow?（疑問）
We won't go shopping tomorrow.（否定）

1. **will** ― 未来、意志、習慣、依頼、指示などの意味があります。
   It will be rainy tomorrow.
   Accidents will happen.（事故は注意しても起こるものだ。（習慣））
2. **must** ― 話し手が課した義務、必要、強い推量の意味があります。
   All passengers must fasten their seatbelts.
3. **have to** ― 規則や状況から判断された義務の意味があります。
   You have to speak only English during this workshop.
   Does he have to speak English during the meeting?
   You don't have to speak English when you answer questions.

Exercise C

日本語を参考に（　　　）に入る語句を上の助動詞から選んで答えましょう。

1. 私達の次の会議は火曜日の午後３時に開かれます。
   Our next meeting (　　　　　　) be held on Tuesday at 3 p.m.
2. その赤ちゃんは何も食べようとしないので、私は少し心配だ。
   The baby (　　　　　　) not eat anything, so I am a bit worried.
3. あなたは 10 月からより高い消費税を払わなくてはならないでしょう。
   You will (　　　　　　) pay a higher consumption tax from October.
4. まず最初にバターと小麦粉を混ぜなくてはいけません。
   First of all, you (　　　　　　) mix the butter with the flour.
5. すべての外国人訪問客はパスポート検査窓口に立ち寄らねばならない。
   All international visitors (　　　　　　) stop at passport control.

Exercise D

日本語を参考に、左の助動詞を使って ……… の部分を英語に直しましょう。モデルパラグラフも参考にすること。

1. その会社は次の数週間で新しい商品を世に出すでしょう。

   This company ....

2. 私達はお年寄りのニーズに合ったより進化したテクノロジーを作り上げねばなりません。

   We ....

3. 英語を流暢に話すのを学ぶことは難しいに違いありません。

   It ....

4. 次の段階は個人情報を与えることです。

   The next step ....

5. 空港への道を教えてくれませんか。

   .... the airport?

Useful Vocabulary

Exercise E

次の語の定義を a. から j. の中から選んで、記号で答えましょう。

_____ 1. entrepreneur
_____ 2. innovator
_____ 3. found
_____ 4. launch
_____ 5. unique
_____ 6. ship (v)
_____ 7. overseas
_____ 8. available
_____ 9. delivery
_____ 10. specify

a. to start something such as an organization, company, or school, often by providing the necessary money
b. to send goods somewhere by ship, plane, truck, etc.
c. to start something, usually something big or important
d. someone who introduces changes and new ideas
e. the act of bringing goods, letters, etc. to a particular person or place, or the things that are brought
f. to or in a foreign country that is across the sea
g. unusually good and special, being the only one of its kind
h. to state something in an exact and detailed way
i. someone who starts a new business or arranges business deals in order to make money, often in a way that involves financial risks
j. to be used or can easily be bought or found

Outline

自分の好きな有名人や偉人を一人取り上げ、その人の生涯について調べ、それについて説明する paragraph の outline を作成してみましょう。

Topic	
Supporting idea ① (event, fact, etc.)	
Supporting idea ② (event, fact, etc.)	
Supporting idea ③ (event, fact, etc.)	
Conclusion	

Writing

上の outline をもとに、取り上げた有名人や偉人の生涯を説明する paragraph を書いてみましょう。

UNIT 7 様々なものを分類してみよう（Classification）

多種多様なものを説明する際、それらを分類して説明すると分かりやすくなります。このunitでは以下の点を目標とします。

- Classificationのparagraphの構造を理解し、よく使われる表現・語彙を学ぶ。
- Classificationのparagraphのoutlineを作成し、完成する。
- Modal（can, may）について学習し、理解する。

Warm Up

A. 次の質問に答えましょう。

1. What type of a person are you?

2. What type of a person do you think the person next to you is?

3. In terms of character, do you two have any similarities?

4. And how about any differences between you two? What are they?

B. 上の質問の答えを隣同士で見せ合い、話し合ってみましょう。

Paragraph Analysis

多種多様なものを説明する際、雑然と説明してしまうと読者に混乱を生じさせます。まずは共通のものを探し、それらをグループ化し、他のグループとの差異に言及し、時として具体例を挙げるとさらに分かりやすくなります。

＜ Useful Expressions ＞

We classify ～ into three groups, ～ is divided [categorized] into four types, ～ consists of ...,
The first group, The second type, An example of the group ～, such as ～, include ～

Exercise A

次の paragraph を読み、以下の質問に答えましょう。

According to a recent study, we all fall into four groups. People classified as "reserved" are typically not very open, but are emotionally stable. At the same time they can be pleasant and responsible at work. (①) group is "role models". Those who belong to this category are usually older. They may be dependable and accept new ideas. It is interesting to note that more women than men are likely to be role models. The (②) group is "self-centered". Self-centered people are usually very open but not always responsible or pleasant. You probably would not want to become friends with someone in this group. (③), some people are just "average". They are not especially open and can be a bit selfish. As you may have guessed, most of us are in this group.

1. 上の paragraph の main idea は何ですか？

2. 上の paragraph 中の（ ）に入る適切な語を下から選びましょう。

   a. also b. third c. second d. importantly e. another f. finally g. other

3. 上の paragraph の趣旨に沿って、下の表に人間のタイプを分類してみましょう。

Type				
Character				

Additional Explanation				

Exercise B

次の paragraph を読み、以下の質問に答えましょう。

As science advances, we discover new sources of energy. However, even today, our energy can be (①) three types. (②) of all, we continue to rely on fossil fuels. This is a traditional source of energy and it (③) coal, oil and natural gas. Fossil fuels may cause pollution and experts predict that at some point in the future fossil fuels will run out. Many countries (④) use nuclear energy. While it is relatively inexpensive, it can be dangerous, especially in the case of an accident or a natural disaster. (⑤), renewable energy, (⑥) solar, wind or hydro power, can be both environmentally friendly and long-lasting. The problem, however, is that at present these energy sources are not very efficient and can be expensive. Today each country must carefully consider its energy policy in the light of national priorities.

1. 上の paragraph の main idea は何ですか？
2. Useful Expressions を参考に、上の paragraph 中の（　）に適切な語（句）を入れましょう。
3. 上の paragraph の趣旨に沿って、下の表にエネルギーの種類を分類してみましょう。

Name of energy			
Explanation			
Examples			

Grammar for Writing

Modals 2 (can, may)

Modal（助動詞）は、Unit 6でも学習したように、話し手の判断などの心的態度を示す品詞で、動詞の原形が続きます。疑問文、否定文での語順はwillの場合と同様です。

1. can — 能力、可能、許可などの意味があります。
   It can be divided into three types.
   Those people can be a bit selfish.（それらの人々は少し自己中心的になることもあります。（可能））
   cf. cannot 〜のはずがない

2. may — 許可、推量の意味があります。
   They may be dependable.（彼らは頼りになるかもしれません。（推量））

Exercise C

日本語を参考に与えられた語句を並び替えましょう。（文頭に来る語も小文字で始めています。）

1. 彼が将来医者になるなんていうことがあり得るでしょうか。
   (he / in the future / can / a doctor / become)?

2. もう少しあとで彼の事務所を訪ねるようにしてもいいですよ。
   (visit / may / later / try to / his office / a bit / you).

3. 車を借りればあなたはどこへでも行けます。
   (go / want / you / a car / you / anywhere / rent / you / if / can).

4. 12月にもう一度この試験を受けることができます。
   (can / in December / this exam / try to / you / again / take).

5. シカゴの中心街を詳しく案内してくれたので、彼女は建築家かもしれません。
   (because / us / she / downtown Chicago / such a thorough tour / an architect / she / be / of / may / gave).

Exercise D

日本語を参考に、左ページにある助動詞を使って ……. の部分を英語に直しましょう。

1. テレビに出ているので、彼女はここにいるはずがありません。

   ________ because I am seeing her on TV.

2. 本当にそうするつもりならメジャー（専攻科目）を変えてもいいですよ。

   ________ if you are really determined to do it.

3. 証拠から考えると、彼の説明は正しいのかもしれません。

   Considering the evidence, ________.

4. 彼女はマイク（Mike）にとてもよく似ているので彼の姉ということもあり得ます。

   ________ because she looks so much like him.

5. 雨がやむまでロビーにいてもいいよ。

   ________ until it stops raining.

Useful Vocabulary

Exercise E

次の語（句）の定義を a. から j. の中から選んで、記号で答えましょう。

____ 1. reserved
____ 2. typically
____ 3. role model
____ 4. predict
____ 5. run out
____ 6. relatively
____ 7. renewable
____ 8. hydro
____ 9. long-lasting
____ 10. dependable

a. to be replaced naturally or controlled carefully and can therefore be used without the risk of finishing it all
b. a person looked by others as an example to be imitated
c. to a fairly large degree, especially in comparison to something else
d. in the way that a particular type of thing usually happens
e. trustworthy and reliable
f. continuing for a long time
g. to be used up; to be consumed
h. slow or unwilling to show feelings or express opinions
i. relating to water
j. to say that something will happen in the future

Outline

分類したいものを考え、そのそれぞれの種類について下の表を完成させましょう。

Topic				
Type (Group)				
Explanation				
Examples				

Writing

上の outline をもとに、classification の paragraph を書いてみましょう。

UNIT 8 デジタルとアナログを比較してみよう（Comparison and Contrast）

ある一つの事柄を他の事柄と比較する場合は、類似点を中心に書きます。対照させる場合には、相違点に着目して書きます。二つの事象の類似点・相違点を明らかにすることで自分の考えや主張を論理的に示すことができます。この unit では以下の点を到達目標とします。

- Comparison and Contrast の paragraph の構造を理解し、よく使われる表現・語彙を学ぶ。
- Comparison and Contrast の paragraph の outline を作成し、完成する。
- Modal（would, could, might）について学び、その表現上の特徴を理解する。

Warm Up

A. 他のクラスメイトに、電子書籍を読んだことがあるか（Have you ever read an e-book?）、何について書かれた本だったのか（What kind of a book did you read?)、紙の本と電子書籍のどちらが好きか（Which do you like better, paper books or e-books?）について質問し、その理由も聞いて、メモを取ってみましょう。

Question: ....

Answer: ....

Question: ....

Answer: ....

Question: ....

Answer: ....

B. 上のメモにもとづいて、読んだことのある電子書籍を他のクラスメイトに英語で簡単に紹介してみましょう。

Paragraph Analysis

比較・対照 (Comarison and Contrast) の paragraph とは、二つの事柄の類似点、相違点を説明していく paragraph です。例えば、二つの事柄のうちどちらが望ましいのか、自分の意見を説得力のある形で示すために、この比較・対照のパラグラフ構成を用います。主観的な好き嫌いではなく、両者の良い点、悪い点を列挙させながら自分の意見や主張をまとめていくことができます。私たちの日常生活においても学術論文の構成でも比較・対照の思考方法は重要です。

＜Useful Expressions＞

類似を表す表現：resemble（と似ている), be similar to ～（～に似ている), like（のように),
the same ... as ～（～と同じ）

相違を表す表現：differ from（と異なっている), be different from（と違う), unlike（と違って）

二つの句や節を対照的に結びつける副詞(句)には次のようなものがあります。：however（しかしながら), on the other hand（一方では), in contrast（対照的に）

二つの文や節を対照的に結びつける接続詞には次のようなものがあります。：but（しかし), while（一方), although（にもかかわらず), though（だが), whereas（いっぽうで、だけれども）

Exercise A

次の paragraph を読み、以下の質問に答えましょう。

A few decades ago, if you wanted to read something, you had to buy a real book or a magazine. Today, we have a choice: we can purchase a paper copy or a digital copy of the same novel. And these days more and more people prefer to read e-books. They offer many benefits. First of all, they take up no space. You can carry hundreds of books in one small machine. Another important advantage is that e-books tend to be much cheaper. Sometimes you can download them for free. The good point of paper books, on the other hand, is that reading them does not hurt your eyes as much. Additionally, you do not have to worry about your battery running out. Finally, some people simply like to hold a real book in hand when they read. So, there are fans of both types of books. Which one do you prefer?

1. 上の paragraph の main idea は何ですか？ 一文を書き抜きましょう。
2. 上の paragraph で対照を際立たせる表現は何ですか？ 下線を引いてみましょう。
3. 上の paragraph の趣旨に沿って、以下の表を完成させましょう。最初の空欄は埋めてあります。

The good points of e-books
E-books take up no space.

The good points of paper books
Reading paper books does not hurt your eyes.

Exercise B

次の paragraph を読み、以下の質問に答えましょう。

Until quite recently the only way to translate a document was to ask a specialist. However, today there is an ongoing debate: should we rely on a human or a computer for this important task? While the quality of machine translation has improved significantly, it is still not at the level performed by a live person. Translation software often cannot understand the creative use of language or expressions specific to a particular culture. In terms of speed and cost, on the other hand, machine translation offers obvious advantages. There are many free applications available which can translate pages of text in a matter of minutes. These applications can translate an announcement into 25 different languages, something that would require several human translators. So, I believe, if you insist on an accurate translation, human skill is still the best but if efficiency is more important, machine translation offers us a solution.

1. 上の paragraph の main idea は何ですか？ 一文を書き抜きましょう。
2. 上の paragraph で対照を際立たせる表現は何ですか？ 下線を引いてみましょう。
3. 上の paragraph の趣旨に沿って、machine translation の良い点、悪い点を書いてみましょう。

The benefits of machine translation
The drawbacks of machine translation

Grammar for Writing

Modals 2 (would, could, might)

Modal（助動詞）の過去形は、基本的には過去のことではなく、丁寧さや低い可能性を表します。もともと助動詞の過去形は仮定法で用いられていたので、「もし～できたら」の意味が加わることで、丁寧さが含意されます。また、現在や過去の事実に反する内容を表す仮定法では、実現の可能性が低いことになります。二つの表現の丁寧さの度合いも考えてみましょう。

Can I borrow this dictionary? / Could I borrow this dictionary?
Will you tell me the way to the university? / Would you tell me the way to the university?

I would like to call a taxi. などの would like to「したい」という意味も丁寧な表現であるとわかると思います。

1. would ―習慣、依頼、指示などの意味があります。
   She would often go shopping with her mother.（母親と一緒に彼女は買い物に行ったものでした。）
   Would you open the window?（窓を開けていただけますか。）

2. could ― 許可、依頼、低い可能性の意味があります。
   You could ask him.（彼に聞いてもいいと思います。）
   Could I have another cup of tea, please? （もう一杯お茶をいただけますか。）
   He could be famous.（彼は有名になるかもしれません。[でもなれないでしょう]）

3. might ― 低い可能性・推量や許可の意味があります。
   He might actually come earlier.（彼は早く来るかもしれないよ。）
   It might be a good idea to stop at an ATM and take out some money.
   （ATM に寄ってお金を引き出すのはいい考えかもしれません。）

Exercise C

日本語を参考に（　　　）に入る語句を上の助動詞から選んで答えましょう。

1. 5 才だったとき、息子はバイオリンを弾くことができました。
   My son (　　　　　) play the violin when he was five.
2. 彼女は飛行機に乗っているか、搭乗中でしょう。というのも彼女の携帯電話の電源が切られているから。
   She (　　　　　) be on the plane, or boarding, because her mobile phone is switched off.
3. 高校時代にはよくテニスをしたものです。
   I (　　　　　) play tennis when I was at high school.
4. ぜひあなたにいつかオックスフォードを訪問してほしいのです。
   I (　　　　　) like you to visit Oxford someday.
5. よろしければ家族写真を送っていただけますでしょうか。
   (　　　　　) you possibly send me a photo of your family?

Exercise D

日本語を参考に、助動詞を使って .... の部分を英語に直しましょう。

1. 名前を教えてくれますか。

   ....?

2. 財布をなくしてしまったかもしれません。

   ....

3. 父はおそらく家に帰ってくるでしょう。

   My father ....

4. フロリダに住んでいたときには、週末には海岸によく行ったものでした。

   We ....

5 お飲み物はいかがですか。

   ....?

Useful Vocabulary

Exercise E

次の語の定義を a. から j. の中から選んで、記号で答えましょう。

____ 1. decade
____ 2. offer
____ 3. purchase
____ 4. copy
____ 5. benefit
____ 6. advantage
____ 7. magazine
____ 8. worry
____ 9. hurt
____ 10. battery

a. one of many books, magazines, records etc.
b. an object that provides a supply of electricity for something such as a radio, car, or toy
c. to ask someone if they would like to have something
d. a large thin book with a paper cover that contains news stories, articles, photographs etc, and is sold weekly or monthly
e. to injure yourself or someone else
f. a period of 10 years
g. something that helps you to be more successful than others, or the state of having this
h. to be anxious or unhappy about someone or something, so that you think about them a lot
i. an advantage, improvement, or help that you get from something
j. to buy something

Outline

自分の好きな絵本や本を二冊取り上げ、類似点、相違点を調べ、それについて説明する paragraph の Outline を書いてみましょう。

Book 1: title ....

Book 2: title ....

Topic	
Supporting idea ① (story, character, etc.)	
Supporting idea ② (story, character, etc.)	
Supporting idea ③ (story, character, etc.)	
Conclusion	

Writing

上の outline をもとに、自分の選んだ二冊の本を紹介する paragraph を書いてみましょう。

UNIT 9 原因と結果を明らかにしよう(Cause and Effect)

原因（Cause）と結果（Effect）を明らかにする因果関係は、paragraph に論理的な説得力を持たせます。この unit では以下の点を到達目標とします。

・ Cause and Effect の paragraph の構造を理解し、よく使われる表現・語彙を学ぶ。
・ Cause and Effect の paragraph の outline を作成し、完成する。
・ 句や節を対等に結びつける等位接続詞（Coordinating Conjunctions）について学び、その機能上の特徴を理解する。

Warm Up

A. 人口減少がもたらす問題点（Drawbacks）と良い点（Benefits）について自分なりに考え、下の表に書きこんでみましょう。

Effects (Drawbacks)
・ (Ex.) The number of taxpayers will decrease.
・
・
・
・
Effects (Benefits)
・(Ex.) With a smaller population, Japan's natural environment will be less polluted.
・
・
・
・

B. 自分が挙げた人口減少の drawbacks と benefits について互いに紹介し、意見を交換し合いましょう。

Paragraph Analysis

因果関係を述べる paragraph は、ある事象についてその結果と原因を明らかにする paragraph です。学術論文の構成においては、ある事象の原因と結果を明らかにすることによって論理性が高まりますし、日常の事柄の選択においても必然性が理解できるようになります。ただし、その原因と結果の因果関係の度合いが論理性を左右しますので気を付けてください。例えば、「昨日雨が降っていたので路面がぬれている」と「昨日雨が降ったので、風邪をひいてしまった」では因果関係に程度差があります。後者では読み手に何らかの推量（雨に濡れたせいで、体が冷えたので風邪をひいてしまった）が必要な点で直接的な論理性が弱まります。このタイプの paragraph では、まず説明すべき事象を取り上げ、その原因を詳細に説明してから、結果と事象の重要性について述べるようにします。

＜ Useful Expressions ＞

このタイプの paragraph で用いられる表現には以下のようなものがあります。

原因（主語）が結果（目的語）に至る意味の動詞：cause（を引き起こす）, result in（結果として…になる）, lead to（に至る）, bring about（もたらす）

原因である名詞句を導く前置詞句：because of（のために）, as a result of（の結果として）, due to（のせいで）, thanks to（のおかげで）, owing to（によって）

結果を導く前置詞句と副詞：as a result（結果として…）, in consequence（結果として）, therefore（それゆえに）, consequently（結果的に）

Exercise A

次の paragraph を読み、以下の質問に答えましょう。

Birthrate decline in Japan is probably one of the most serious problems the country is facing today. According to some experts, the population of Japan may fall below 100 million by 2060. Such a drastic decline will have a number of serious effects. First of all, as the working population decreases, national production and consumption will drop. Most importantly, the percentage of elderly people in society will certainly rise. As a result, medical and other social costs will go up, while the number of taxpayers will be getting smaller and smaller. The government may not have enough money to pay pensions and provide the necessary services. As you can see, a low birthrate poses a risk to the economic and social future of the country.

1. 上の paragraph の main idea は何ですか？
2. 上の paragraph で列挙を示す表現は何ですか？
3. 上の paragraph で述べられている出生率に伴う原因と結果について、次のページの表を完成させましょう。

Part II

Causes	Effects
The working population decreases.	
The percentage of elderly people in society will certainly rise.	
The number of taxpayers will be getting smaller and smaller.	

Exercise B

次の paragraph を読み、以下の質問に答えましょう。 17

These days, we often see media reports about university students suffering from stress. While this is due to many possible factors, we can identify several key causes. First of all, students may have difficulty adjusting to a new environment. This is especially true in the case of those who move to another city for their studies. Secondly, some students may not be able to keep up with their school work. Course material can be pretty advanced, and classes tend to be large. As a result, students have to spend a lot of time reviewing their notes and preparing. Finally, a large number of students do not have a healthy lifestyle. They don't exercise enough, skip breakfast, and often try to get by on only a few hours of sleep a night. It is very important to understand what causes stress in order to find ways to reduce its impact on us.

1. 上の paragraph で main idea は何ですか？
2. 上の paragraph 中で main idea を言い換えている文を抜き出してみましょう。
3. 上の paragraph で述べられている大学生のストレスに伴う原因と結果について、下の表を完成させましょう。

Causes	Effects
Students move to another city for their studies.	
	Some students may not be able to keep up with their school work.
	A large number of students do not have a healthy lifestyle.

Grammar for Writing

Coordinating Conjunction（等位接続詞）は、語と語、句と句、節と節を対等に結んでいます。用法は以下のように分類されます。何と何が対等な関係なのかに気を付けてください。

1. addition（添加）——— It is sunny today, and very humid.
2. alternative（代替）— We can go out tonight, or we can stay home and watch a movie.
3. contrast（対照）——— It is rainy today, but yesterday the weather was great.
4. adversative（譲歩）— Though it's rainy today, we have decided to go on a picnic.
5. reason（理由）——— We are going to stay home, because it's supposed to rain all day.
6. consequence（結果）— It's been raining all today, so we decided to stay home.

Exercise C

日本語を参考に（　　　）に適切な接続詞を入れましょう。

1. 私がメアリーを見ると、彼女も私を見ました。
   I saw Mary, (　　　　　　) she saw me.
2. 彼は幸せそうだが、悩みを抱えています。
   He seems happy, (　　　　　　) he is going through some rough time.
3. 雨が降っていたので、試合は延期になりました。
   It was raining, (　　　　　　) the game was called off.
4. もっと勉強しないと試験に落ちてしまうよ。
   You have to put more time into study, (　　　　　　) you will fail the exam.
5. 彼を信用していた、というのも親友だったので。
   I trusted him, (　　　　　　) he was my closest friend.

Exercise D

日本語を参考に、接続詞を用いて .... の部分を英語に直しましょう。

1. この論文は有益で、さらに面白いです。

   This article is ....
2. 私はコーヒーも紅茶もどちらも好きではありません。

   I don't like either ....

3. 彼らも私も８時のバスに間に合いませんでした。

Neither ____.

4. 学生だけでなく教授も間違っていました。

Not only ____.

5 準備に時間をかけなさい。そうすれば試験に受かりますよ。

Spend more time preparing, ____.

Useful Vocabulary

Exercise E

次の語の定義を a. から j. の中から選んで、記号で答えましょう。

____ 1. serious
____ 2. face
____ 3. expert
____ 4. population
____ 5. drastic
____ 6. decline
____ 7. consumption
____ 8. government
____ 9. pension
____ 10. pose

a. to accept that a difficult situation or problem exists, even though you would prefer to ignore it
b. the number of people living in a particular area, country etc.
c. the group of people who govern a country or state
d. important and needing a lot of thought or attention
e. to exist in a way that may cause a problem, danger, difficulty etc.
f. the act of buying and using products
g. an amount of money paid regularly by the government or company to someone who does not work anymore, for example because they have reached the age when people stop working or because they are ill
h. extreme and sudden
i. a decrease in the quality, quantity, or importance of something
j. someone who has a special skill or special knowledge of a subject, gained as a result of training or experience

Outline

SNS(Social Network Service) の普及が若い人々の精神状態 (mental health) にどのような影響を与えているでしょうか。原因と結果を示しながら下の表に書き出してみましょう。

Causes	Effects

Writing

上の outline をもとに、SNS(Social Network Service) の普及が若い人々の精神状態 (mental health) にどのような影響を与えているか paragraph を書いてみましょう。

UNIT 10 問題に対する解決策を考えてみよう (Problem-Solution)

ある問題に対し、解決策を論理的に提示する paragraph 構造です。問題の重要性と説得力のある解決策の表現方法がポイントになります。この unit では以下の点を到達目標とします。

- Problem-Solution の paragraph の構造を理解し、よく使われる表現・語彙を学ぶ。
- Problem-Solution の paragraph の outline を作成し、完成する。
- 名詞節や副詞節を導く従属接続詞 (Subordinating Conjunctions) について学び、その機能上の特徴を理解する。

Warm Up

A. 次の質問に答えましょう。

1. Why do you study English?

2. How do you study English now?

3. What are some of the problems of learning English after entering university? What solutions can you suggest?

4. What foreign language do you want to study?

B. 上の質問の答えを隣同士で見せ合い、話し合ってみましょう。

Paragraph Analysis

問題―解決の paragraph 構造ではまず、問題が何か、現状分析を踏まえて解決しなくてはいけない問題であることを示します。そこに統計的な数値や歴史的背景を加え、問題の意義を明らかにすることも可能です。次にその解決策として実行可能なもの、また代替策をいくつか示し、結論部で最適な解決策を説明することになります。

＜ Useful Expressions ＞

問題の提示： The problem is that ..., One of the main problems is ..., Another major problem is ...,

問題の実例： For example, ..., For instance, ...,

問題の結果： There is no doubt that ..., resulting in ...,

解決策の提示： In terms of solutions, I believe ..., To solve the problem, we should (must, need to) ...,

解決策の列挙： Firstly, Secondly, Finally, The first solution is that ..., The second solution is that ...,

Exercise A

次の paragraph を読み、以下の質問に答えましょう。

University entrance exams in Japan are extremely important. Unfortunately, after passing the exams, students often lose motivation to study. Then, what's a good strategy to maintain motivation to study English once the difficult exams are behind us? I would like to offer a few suggestions. (　　　　), try to have fun studying English. Perhaps you enjoy watching American movies or listening to British pop songs. Here is your opportunity to improve your listening skills. (　　　　) idea is to become friends with someone who is very interested in English. This way, you can help and encourage each other as you struggle to improve your skills. Get to know some foreign students and learn about their culture by communicating in English. Most (　　　　), try to think of how English can be of use to you in the future. Keep in mind, language study does not end with the entrance exams.

1. 上の paragraph の main idea は何ですか？

2. 上の paragraph 中の（　）に入る適切な語を下から選びましょう。

   a. First of all　b. Thirdly　c. Secondly　d. importantly　e. Another　f. finally　g. other

3. 上の paragraph の趣旨に沿って、英語で筆者の解決案を書き出してみましょう。

Exercise B

次の paragraph を読み、以下の質問に答えましょう。

One of the challenges young people face is planning their professional lives. It can be very difficult to decide what we want to do in the future. To make this process a little easier, it is a good idea to follow these steps. First of all, make a list of activities which you enjoy. For example, do you like travelling? How about communicating with people, or working with animals? Then, think of professions which involve these activities. If you are not sure, ask your friends, parents or the school counsellor. Once you narrow down the range of possible jobs, you can begin to think of the additional skills you need to acquire. This step is critical because it will give you an idea of what you should study at college, what internships you should consider and whether you need to get some qualifications. Designing your future career may be a bit scary but it's certainly necessary.

1. 上の paragraph の main idea は何ですか？
2. 上の paragraph 中の these steps は何を指しているでしょうか。具体的に英語で書き出してみましょう。
3. 上の paragraph の趣旨に沿って、自分たちで考えた解決策について評価をする部分を書き足してみましょう。

Grammar for Writing

Subordinating Conjunction（従属接続詞）は、節を名詞や副詞と同じ役割に変えます。名詞節では文の一部として主語や目的語、補語になります。副詞節では時、理由、条件、譲歩などを表します。用法は以下のように分類されます。

1. 名詞節を導く従属接続詞 ― **that, if, whether**
   I think that he is rich.　彼は金持ちだと思っています。＝目的語
   The question is whether he is rich.　問題は、彼が金持ちかどうかということです。＝補語

2. 副詞節を導く従属接続詞 ― **when, while, as, before, after, until, since, because, if, unless, though, although**
   When I was a junior high school student, I belonged to a tennis club.
   If it were not for water, we could not survive.

   副詞節を導く接続表現 ― **as soon as, every time, so ... that ～, so that ... can, in case, as far as, as long as**
   I will tell you what happened as soon as you get here.

Exercise C

日本語を参考に（　　　）に適切な接続詞を入れましょう。

1. 彼は歩き回ってようやく家につきました。
   He walked and walked (　　　　　) at last he came home.

2. いい天気だから、散歩でもしましょう。
   (　　　　　) it is such a beautiful day, let's take a walk.

3. 雨が降らない限りはお迎えに伺います。
   I will pick you up (　　　　　) it rains.

4. 努力はしたのですが、試験には落ちてしまいました。
   (　　　　　) I studied a lot , I didn't do well on the exam.

5. いったん、発音の仕方を覚えてしまえば、忘れません。
   (　　　　　) you learn how to pronounce it, you never forget.

Exercise D

日本語を参考に、接続詞を用いて .... の部分を英語に直しましょう。

1. 部屋を出る前にスイッチを消してください。

   Please turn off the light ______________________________ .

2. たとえ明日が雨でも、買い物には行きます。

   ______________________________, we'll go shopping.

3. 私に関する限り、質問はありません。

   ______________________________, everything is clear.

4. 手伝っていただけないでしょうか。

   ______________________________ you could help me.

5 彼がそうするのは当たり前です。

   ______________________________ he would act in this way.

Useful Vocabulary

Exercise E

次の語の定義を a. から j. の中から選んで、記号で答えましょう。

____ 1. motivation
____ 2. strategy
____ 3. suggestion
____ 4. fun
____ 5. opportunity
____ 6. encourage
____ 7. struggle
____ 8. improve
____ 9. skill
____ 10. entrance

a. a planned series of actions for achieving something
b. a chance to do something or an occasion when it is easy for you to do something
c. to make something better, or to become better
d. an ability to do something well, especially because you have learned and practiced it
e. to give someone the courage or confidence to do something
f. to try extremely hard to achieve something, even though it is very difficult
g. eagerness and willingness to do something without needing to be told or forced to do it
h. the right or ability to go into a place
i. enjoyable and amusing
j. an idea, plan, or possibility that someone mentions, or the act of mentioning it

Outline

Nowadays pretty much everyone has a laptop, and a large number of children spend their weekends playing computer games.
What are the drawbacks of playing computer games and what can be done to minimize the adverse effect?

Writing

上の outline をもとに、problem-solution の paragraph を書いてみましょう。

UNIT 11 Paragraph to Presentation (Introduction)

Unit 11 では Introduction について学習し、それを 5 つの観点から分析します。そしてこれまで書いてきたパラグラフをプレゼンテーションに向けて構成していく方法を学んでいきます。まず、プレゼンテーションの構造について簡単に説明していきます。プレゼンテーションの目的は、自分の主張を聞き手にわかりやすく、正確に伝えるということです。そのためには、発表者と聞き手が共有すべきプレゼンテーションの構造に基づいて、原稿やパワーポイントを準備しなくてはいけません。

プレゼンテーションの基本構造は次の通りです。大きく Introduction − Body − Conclusion の三つの部分に分かれ、さらに下記のように区分されます。

Introduction	Greetings	挨拶
	Introducing yourself	自己紹介
	Introducing the topic	話題の導入
	Introducing the main idea	主張の導入
	Starting the presentation	開始の合図
Body	Point	要点の提示
	Explanation	要点の説明
	Examples = Facts, Figures	要点を支える実例、数字
	Repeating the point	要点の繰り返し
Conclusion	Summarizing	要約
	Repeating the main point	主張の繰り返し
	Expressing your feeling of gratitude	聞き手への謝意
	Showing references	参考文献の提示
	Informing the audience of your contact information	連絡先
	Inviting questions and comments	質疑応答

まず、Unit10 の Model Paragraph をプレゼンテーション用に加筆したものを読んでみましょう。

(Introduction)

Hello, everyone. I am a student at Nan'un University majoring in linguistics. Thanks for coming here today. The objective of today's presentation is to share with you my ideas about how you can improve your English at university. In this talk, I would like to suggest ways to maintain our motivation to learn English. We all know that entrance exams in Japan are extremely important. Unfortunately, after passing the exams, we often lose motivation to study. Then, what's a good strategy to keep going? This presentation may offer some ideas. So, let me begin.

(Body)

First of all, try to have fun studying English. Perhaps you enjoy watching American movies or listening to British pop songs. Here is your opportunity to improve your listening skills. Another idea is to become friends with someone who is very interested in English. This way, you can help and encourage each other as you struggle to improve your skills. Get to know some foreign students and learn about their culture by communicating in English. It goes without saying that if you have an opportunity to study overseas your English skills will improve dramatically. I understand that many of you are a bit reluctant to leave your friends and family behind. So, why not start with a short-term program? How about staying abroad for just a week or two? You will be surprised how much confidence you will gain after just a short stay in an English-speaking country. Most importantly, try to think of how English can be of use to you in the future. Keep in mind, language study does not end with the entrance exams.

(Conclusion)

All the ideas I mentioned today are very realistic and in my opinion, effective to give you real-life opportunities to listen to and speak the language. Remember, language study should be a lifelong pursuit. In fact, this is just the beginning of your linguistic journey! Thank you very much for your attention. Here are some useful websites. If you would like to know more, don't hesitate to contact me. My email is on the last slide. At this point, I am happy to take any questions or comments you may have.

Introduction を５つの観点から分析してみましょう。

1. 挨拶（Greetings）

Hello, everyone.

まずプレゼンテーションでは、目の前に聴衆がいます。彼らに対面して、一般的な挨拶から始めましょう。聴衆全体に目を向け、見渡すように自信をもって大きな声で挨拶をします。挨拶はコミュケーションの基礎の基礎です。ここで背筋を伸ばして大きな声が出るように調整する意味もあります。

2. 自己紹介（Introducing yourself）

I am a student at Nan'un University.

挨拶に続けて、発表者の自己紹介です。名前と所属、もしくは学生であれば専攻を加えるのもいいでしょう。ここまでは原稿に目を落としたり、プレゼンテーションの画面を見ないようにしましょう。

3. 話題の導入（Introducing the topic）

The objective (aim; goal) of today's presentation is to share with you my ideas about how to improve your English at university. We all know that college entrance exams in Japan are extremely important. Unfortunately, after passing the exams, students often lose motivation to study.

プレゼンテーションで、何について話すのか話題を提示します。まず名詞句で簡潔に表題にあたる話題を提示し、その話題を選んだ理由と背景、歴史、現状の分析を続けます。

4. 主張の導入（Introducing main idea）

Then, what's a good strategy to maintain motivation to study English once the difficult exams are behind us? This presentation offers a few suggestions.

話題の提示に対して、先に結論に近い内容を示してプレゼンテーションの全体像を示します。これによって、画面上にあるアウトラインの説明に移ることができます。

5. 開始の合図（Starting the presentation）

So, let me begin.

ここまでは原稿を読まなくても聴衆の前で話せるはずです。次にプレゼンテーションの Body に移るわけですが、聴衆の目をプレゼンテーションの画面に向けるためにも、プレゼンテーションの開始を宣言します。ただ、画面を見てもらうだけでなく、項目を読み上げてもいいでしょう。

Language for Presentation

ここでは introduction のパートでよく用いられる表現を学習しましょう。

1. 挨拶
   Hello, my name is ...
   Hello, everybody.
   Good morning. / Good afternoon. / Good evening. I'm ...

2. 自己紹介
   I work for ... / I represent
   I major in ... / ... My background is in ....
   My name is .... I'm a freshman at ... University, majoring in ....
   Thank you all / Thanks for coming (today).

3. 話題の導入
   Today I'd like to talk about.../ Let me talk about...
   I'm going to introduce.../ Let me introduce ...
   Today I will talk about...
   My topic today is ...
   The topic I chose for this presentation is ...
   From now on, I'm going to talk about ...
   Now I would like to explain ...

4. 主張の導入
   I believe in ...
   Here are my main points. In my presentation I'll share with you some possible solutions.
   By the end of this presentation you will know ...
   There are three things I'd like to address in this presentation.

5. 開始の合図
   This is the outline of my presentation.
   My outline is as follows.
   Let's begin.

Vocabulary for Presentation

Introduction のパートでよく用いられる vocabulary についてチェックしてみましょう。左の語句の意味として適切なものを、右の語群から選びましょう。

____ 1. freshman
____ 2. sophomore
____ 3. junior
____ 4. senior
____ 5. graduate
____ 6. department
____ 7. faculty
____ 8. major
____ 9. focus on
____ 10. aim

a. someone who has completed a university degree, especially a first degree
b. all the teachers in a university
c. the main subject that a student studies at college or university
d. one of the groups of people who work together in a particular part of a large organization such as university
e. a student in the first year of high school or university
f. a student who is in their second year of study at a college or high school
g. a student in the year before the final year of high school or college
h. a student in their last year of high school or university
i. something you hope to achieve by doing something
j. to give special attention to one particular person or thing

Your Own Presentation

Unit 10 で作ったパラグラフ（Problem Solution）の導入部分を、下の構造に従って、またこの unit で学んだ表現を使いながら、自分なりのプレゼンテーション原稿を作ってみましょう。

挨拶：..

....

自己紹介：..

....

話題の導入：..

....

主張の導入：..

....

開始の合図（アウトラインの提示）：..

....

Picture Cards

PowerPoint による提示の仕方について学習しましょう。PowerPoint は Microsoft 社のプレゼンテーション用のソフトで、主として Windows のパソコンで使われます。ここでは PowerPoint でのプレゼンテーションの時に気を付ける点についていくつかあげておきたいと思います。

表示モードをアウトライン表示にしておくとスライドごとのまとめと流れが分かりやすいのでぜひ活用してみてください。また、フッターとヘッダーを活用してページ番号なども表示しておきます。発表時間 1 分にスライド 1 枚、もしくは 2 分に 1 枚程度でかまいません。スライドが多すぎるとプレゼンテーションの内容が聴衆に残りませんので、適当なスライド数を心掛けておいてください。また、スライドにアニメーションをかけすぎたり、画面の切り替え効果に凝りすぎるのも集中力をそいでしまいますので、使いすぎないようにしましょう。

スライドの下のノートに発表原稿を入力することもできますが、これだとパソコンの画面から目が離せなくなりますので、手持ちの紙の原稿か、iPad のような携帯タブレット上にある原稿を見ながら、できるだけ顔を上げて発表を進めるとよいでしょう。

Grammar for Presentation

名詞(Nouns)・形容詞(Adjctives)

名詞は英語の 80%近くを占める品詞です。名詞では一般名詞、集合名詞、抽象名詞、固有名詞などの種類、可算か不可算などのそれぞれの語の持つ意味や特性も知っておかなくてはいけません。また、英語は名詞句、名詞節が一つのまとまりとして主語や目的語になり、文の大きな構成要素になります。英語に特徴的な名詞構文、無生物主語の構文はその例です。

形容詞は名詞を修飾する限定用法や文の補語になる叙述用法の区別、比較級や最上級の活用について気をつけましょう。特に比較・対照はプレゼンテーションでも重要なポイントになりますので、効果的に使ってください。

日本語を参考に与えられた語句を並び替えましょう。(文頭に来る語も小文字で始めています。)

1. 彼は泳ぎが上手です。
   (is / at / he / good / swimming).
2. 雪のために欠航になってしまいました。
   (snowing / , / because / cancelled / was / it / was / flight / my).
3. ひどい雪のせいで私たちは時間通りに出発できませんでした。
   (time / heavy / on / to / for / snow / impossible / it / made / us / leave).
4. 実験のおかげでよい結果が得られました。
   (results / good / experiment / the / showed).
5. 上の図表では用語の定義を示してあります。
   (words / of / illustrate / diagrams / the / definition / the / above).

UNIT

12 Paragraph to Presentation (Body)

Unit 11で学んだintroductionに続いて、このunitでは、プレゼンテーションの中身の部分（Body）について学びます。Bodyでは、まずpointを提示し、要点の説明（Explanation）をし、要点を支える実例、数字などを挙げ（Examples)、要点を繰り返す(Repeating the point)。このunitではconclusionのパートを4つに分けて説明します。まず、unit 10のModel Paragraphのbodyの部分を分析していきたいと思います。

1. まず初めに、目的をはっきり説明しましょう。（下線部①）
   ここでは、suggestions（提案）がされるということがわかります。

2. Point（下線部②）
   ここでは提案がされています。ここでは、transition (first, second, third, finally, etc.)の言葉を使うと、構成がはっきりします。

3. Examples（下線部③）
   ここは下線部②のポイントの具体例あるいは説明です。この具体例の構成をよく見ると3つの具体例があり、それを説明あるいは補強する文章がその後に来ます。

4. Repeating the point（下線部④）
   ここでは、一番初めに言いたかったことを補強して言い換えています。英語を学ぶだけではなく、楽しむことも大切であると（下線部②）初めに書いていますが、次にとにかく英語を学ぶことは将来自分のためにどう役立つか考えることであり、入試や試験で終わるというわけではないといっています。

① So, I would like to offer a few suggestions. ② First of all, try to have fun studying English. ③ Perhaps you enjoy watching American movies or listening to British pop songs. Here is your opportunity to improve your listening skills. Another idea is to become friends with someone who is very interested in English. This way, you can help and encourage each other as you struggle to improve your skills. Get to know some foreign students and learn about their culture by communicating in English. ④ Most importantly, try to think of how English can be of use to you in the future. Keep in mind, language study does not end with the entrance exams.

Language for Presentation

ここではbodyのパートでよく用いられる表現を学習しましょう。

1. 何をするか提示

I would like to offer some suggestions.
I would like to share with you several examples.
I would like to present interesting data.
I will offer a couople of solutions at the end.
I will provide evidence to support my position.
I will present two main arguments.

2. 具体例の提示

具体例を提示するときに、大切なのは、エッセーと違い、音声なので、流れて聞こえてしまうことです。要点や具体例などは、繰り返すかあるいは強調することによって、聞き手に情報をきちんと伝達できます。

Let me repeat the main point.
So what I would like to say here is ...
My main point is ...
Repeating my point, ...

3. 内容の理解の確認

プレゼンテーションの時は聴衆に質問を投げかけたりすることによって、聞き手の状況を確認し、尚且つ、緊張を和らげることができます。

Is my point clear?
Have you ever considered this possibility?
Are you familiar with this topic?

4. 具体例はtransitionを使い、わかりやすくします。

Next, ...
My next point is ...
My other point is ...
Another reason is ...
Another point is ...
Next factor is ...

Exercise A

以下の文章を並び替え body の部分を作成し、ペアで読み合いましょう。

(　　) First, when I went abroad, bringing something Japanese was very useful.

(　　) I would like to share with you several examples.

(　　) Also many people enjoyed taking pictures wearing a yukata.

(　　) I brought along with me some origami and some yukatas.

(　　) When I showed my friends how to make a crane from origami, they were all fascinated by Japanese culture.

(　　) When you go overseas, bringing something Japanese will enhance communication and can help you make a lot of friends.

Vocabulary for Presentation

Exercise B

Body のパートでよく用いられる vocabulary についてチェックしてみましょう。左の語句の意味として適切なものを、右の語群から選びましょう。

_____ 1. opinion
_____ 2. reason
_____ 3. suggestion
_____ 4. crucial
_____ 5. idea
_____ 6. express
_____ 7. statement
_____ 8. characteristic
_____ 9. emphasize
_____ 10. propose

a. to suggest something as a plan or course of action
b. why something happens, or why someone does something
c. an idea, plan, or possibility that someone mentions, or the act of mentioning it
d. a plan for a possible course of action, especially one that you think of suddenly
e. extremely important
f. a quality or feature of something or someone that is typical of them and easy to recognize
g. to say something in a strong way
h. something you say or write, especially publicly or officially, to let people know your intentions or opinions
i. to tell or show what you are feeling or thinking by using words or actions
j. your beliefs about a particular subject

Your Own Presentation

Unit 10 で作ったパラグラフ（Problem Solution）の body の部分を、下の構造に従って、またこの unit で学んだ表現を使いながら、自分なりのプレゼンテーション原稿を作ってみましょう。

段落の目標：

言いたいこと：

具体例：

まとめ（主張）：

Picture Cards

Unit 10 の内容の具体例をパワーポイント風にまとめましょう。内容をまとめるときに様々な方法があります。具体例の場合は、写真を見せたり、箇条書きにしたりと色々と工夫して作ってみてください。

(Example) これは、海外に行くときに持っていくと便利なものをテーマにした発表です。

Slide 1: 箇条書きにポイントを書いているもの

Useful things to take with you when you travel abroad

・Something from your own country

・WiFi to connect to the internet

・Portable battery

Slide 2: 写真

Slide 1

Slide 2

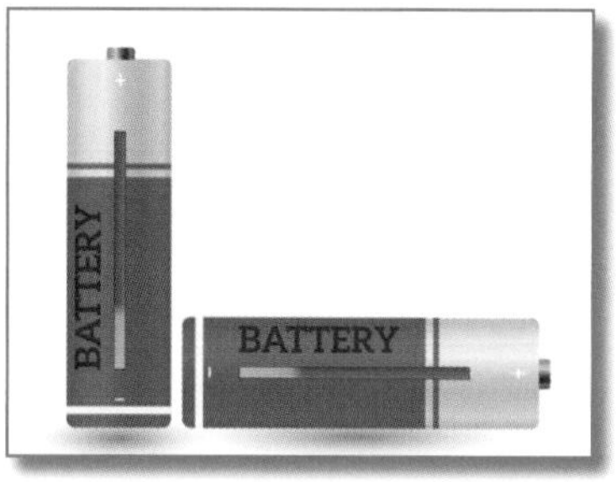

Slide 3

Slide 3: 質問形式

Useful things to take with you when you travel abroad

Part III

Grammar for Presentation

副詞（Adverbs）

ここではadverbs（副詞）に焦点をあてます。副詞は、形容詞と同じ様に、修飾する役割を持っています。ただし形容詞と異なるのは、名詞以外を修飾します。副詞には、２つのパターンがあり、単語の前につくものと、単語の後ろにつくものがあります。

例えば、She is very kind. という文では副詞であるveryは形容詞kindの前についてkindを修飾しています。この前に来る副詞の多くは、程度を表すもの、頻度を表すもの、確信の度合いを表すもの、評価や態度を表すものに分けられます。

例えば、程度を表すものはvery, so, really、頻度を表すものはusually, sometimes, often、確信の度合いを表すものはperhaps, probably, maybe、評価や態度を表すものはhappily, honestly, obviouslyなどがあります。

日本語を参考に、次の文章に当てはまる副詞を入れましょう。

1. 彼女はとても熱心です。
   She is (　　　　　) enthusiastic.
2. 彼は本当に犬好きです。
   He is (　　　　　) a dog lover.
3. 彼女のコミュニケーションスキルはおそらく高いのだろう。
   Her communication skills are (　　　　　) high.
4. 彼はジョンの要望を喜んで受け入れました。
   He (　　　　　) accepted John’s offer.
5. 彼の答えは明らかに間違っています。
   His answer is (　　　　　) wrong.

UNIT 13

Paragraph to Presentation（Conclusion）

これまで introduction、body のパートを学習してきました。この unit では conclusion のパートを学習します。単に conclusion といっても、本格的に行うとなるとなかなか複雑です。言い換えれば、このパートの内容やパフォーマンス次第で、全体のプレゼンテーションの印象が決まるといっても過言ではないでしょう。この unit では conclusion のパートを 6 つに分けて説明します。

Conclusion

① All the ideas I mentioned today are very realistic and in my opinion, effective to give you real-life opportunities to listen to and speak the language. ② Remember, language study should be a lifelong pursuit. In fact, this is just the beginning of your linguistic journey! ③ Thank you very much for your attention. ④ Here are some useful websites. ⑤ If you would like to know more, don't hesitate to contact me. My email is on the last slide. ⑥ At this point, I am happy to take any questions or comments you may have.

① 要約（Summarizing）

ここでは introduction パート、body パートで述べてきた内容を、同じ言葉ではなく、言い換えて簡潔に要約します。

② ポイントを繰り返す（Repeating the main point）

要約だけではプレゼンテーションの内容をまとめただけで、印象には残りません。もう一度このプレゼンテーションを通して何を伝えたかったのかを、一文、もしくは多くても二文程度で、ずばりと表現しましょう。最初に、“Remember,” といった signal word を使うと、聴衆もより耳を傾けるはずです。また、“linguistic journey” といった少し比喩的な表現等も使うと、聴衆の印象に残りやすいです。

③ 聴衆にお礼を言う（Expressing your feeling of gratitude）

長い時間にわたり、自分のプレゼンテーションを聴いてくれた聴衆に対するお礼の言葉を伝えるのも忘れないようにしましょう。

④ 参考文献を示す（Showing references）

論文などでもそうですが、もちろん口頭による発表でも、そこで数字やデータなどを引用した場合は、その数字やデータの出所（出典）を示さなくてはいけません。多くの場合、PowerPoint のスライドやプレゼンテーションを行う際に配るハンドアウト（配布資料）に出典を書いて示しますが、その書き方については後程学びます。

⑤ 自分の連絡先を伝える（Informing the audience of your contact information）

後で質疑応答も行いますが、そこで十分議論し尽くされなかったり、また聴衆の中には大勢の前で質問するのはちょっと…という人もいます。また、ここでの質問のやり取りを通してせっかく築き上げた人間関係を、この場かぎりのものにしてしまうのはもったいないです。後の発展も考えて、ここで自分の電話番号やメールアドレスを示しておくのもよいかもしれません。

⑥ 質問やコメントを受け付ける（Inviting questions and comments）

最後に、自分が行ったプレゼンテーションについて質問やコメントがないかどうか尋ねるのを忘れないで下さい。日本人は概してこの「質疑応答」が苦手ですが、この時間がむしろ重要とみなす人もいます。最初から、“I can’t understand your point.” や “I cannot answer your question now. I want to check at home, so can I contact you later?” と言って質問を避けようとするのではなく（もちろん本当に分からない時はこういった表現は役立ちます）、分かる範囲内で誠意を持って答えれば、あなたに対する印象もずっと良くなるはずです。

Language for Presentation

ここでは特に Conclusion のパートでよく用いられる表現を学習しましょう。

1. 要約（Summarizing）

To summarize, …
In summary, …
In conclusion, …
Now I would like to summarize my presentation.
Let me finish my presentation by summarizing …
Now let me remind you of some of the problems that I have raised.
I would like to go over the points which I have mentioned again.

2. ポイントを繰り返す（Repeating the main point）

Keep in mind that …
Now I would like to remind you of my position.
Now I would like to state my position again.
I believe … should …
After carefully considering all the points, I believe …

3. 聴衆にお礼を言う（Expressing your feeling of gratitude）

Thank you very much for listening.
I really appreciate your time.
I do appreciate your understanding and patience.

4. 参考文献を示す（Showing references）

Here are the sources I have mentioned in this presentation.
Let me show you the URLs for these surveys.
Before concluding my presentation, I would like to show you the references I have consulted.

5. 自分の連絡先を伝える（**Informing the audience of your contact information**）

Here is my contact information, so …

I would appreciate it if you could send whatever questions and comments you have to this address.

6. 質問やコメントを受け付ける（**Inviting questions and comments**）

Do you have any questions or comments?

I will try my best to answer any questions you may have.

There is a lot of time left, so …

We have a few minutes for questions.

We still have several minutes, so …

We have enough time for just one or two more questions.

I'm glad you asked me that.

I'm afraid I don't know …

To be honest with you, I'm not sure …

Let me talk to you later individually.

Let's set up another meeting to discuss that.

Vocabulary for Presentation

Conclusion のパートでよく用いられる vocabulary についてチェックしてみましょう。左の語句の意味として適切なものを、右の語群から選びましょう。

____ 1. conclude
____ 2. summarize
____ 3. contact number
____ 4. position
____ 5. appreciate
____ 6. view
____ 7. refer to
____ 8. attention
____ 9. URL
____ 10. keep in mind

a. to mention something
b. to make a short statement giving only the main information
c. the interest that people show in someone or something
d. to remember or think about someone or something when you are doing something
e. a website address
f. the situation that someone is in, especially when this affects what they can and cannot do
g. to decide that something is true after considering all the information you have
h. to thank someone in a polite way or to say that you are grateful for something they have done
i. a telephone number or address where someone can be found if necessary
j. to think about something or someone in a particular way

Your Own Presentation

Unit 10 で作ったパラグラフ（Problem Solution）の結論部分を、下の構造に従って、またこの unit で学んだ表現を使いながら、自分なりのプレゼンテーション原稿を作ってみましょう。

要約：

ポイントを繰り返す：

聴衆にお礼を言う：

参考文献を示す：

自分の連絡先を伝える：

質問やコメントを受け付ける：

Picture Cards

References（参考文献）の提示の方法について学習しましょう。提示の方法には専門分野によって基本的に定められたスタイルがあります。ここでは、社会科学系分野で最も頻繁に利用される APA スタイルという方法について学びます。

① 本・書籍

例：Yoffe, L., Oku, S., Kakuta, M., Satake, Y., & Morita, A. (2020). *Message Delivered*. Tokyo: Nan'un-do.

「著者の姓 , 著者の名（イニシャルのみ）.（出版年）. 本・書籍のタイトル（イタリック体、手書きの場合は下線を施す）. 出版地 : 出版社名」の順に書く。

② 学術雑誌などの記事

例：Yamada, T. (1990). The effective way of making a presentation. *Business English*, 11(2), 129-158.

「著者の姓 , 著者の名（イニシャルのみ）.（出版年）. 記事のタイトル . 雑誌のタイトル（イタリック体、手書きの場合は下線を施す）, 雑誌の巻数（雑誌の号数）, ページ番号」の順に書く。

③ ウェブサイト

例：Suzuki, H. (2011, August 25). Welcome to Hanako's Room. Retrieved July 25, 2019 from https://sites.abcdefg/hijklmnopqrstu/

「著者の姓 , 著者の名（イニシャルのみ）.（掲載された日付）. ウェブサイトのタイトル . Retrieved 検索した日付 from ウェブサイトの URL」の順に書く。

Grammar for Presentation

命令法（Imperative）

Imperative（命令法）とは、文字通り、命令する際に用いられるものですが、「依頼」の表現も含まれます。プレゼンテーションでは、もちろん presenter が中心となって話すことが多いですが、audience とのやりとりも大切です。そのような時、この命令法がよく使われます。併せてプレゼンテーションの質疑応答でよく用いられる依頼の表現等も学習します。

Please take a look at this graph.
Will you please give us a few examples?
Could you explain a bit more about the relationship between these variables?
（これらの変数の関係についてもう少し説明して頂けませんか。）
I wonder if you could expand on the historical background of this treaty.
（この条約の歴史的背景について詳しく説明して頂けませんか。）

日本語を参考に与えられた語句を並び替えましょう。（文頭に来る語も小文字で始めています。）

1. この現象によって起こり得る影響について皆さんの考えをお聞かせ下さい。
(the possible effects / share / of / on / could / this phenomenon / you / your views)?

2. 私の提案についての皆さんのお考えはいかがですか。
(about / are / my proposal / your thoughts / what)?

3. このグラフが正しくない理由をもう一度説明して頂けませんか。
(why / please / correct / one more time / you / not / can / this graph / explain / is)?

4. さらに２、３個例を挙げて頂けないでしょうか。
(if / a few / I / you / examples / us / with / was wondering / could / additional / provide).

5. カナダとアメリカ合衆国の経済上の関係についてもう少し時間を割いて頂けませんか。
(a little more time / between / spending / mind / the US / the economic relationship / you / Canada / on / and / would)?

UNIT 14

Evaluation

これまでのunitで作ったpresentationを自分たちで評価してみましょう。評価の方法は二つあって、自分で自分のpresentationを評価する自己評価 (Self-evaluation) と、クラスメイトのpresentationを評価し、改善点を指摘するピア・レヴュー (Peer Review/Evaluation) があります。

Self-Evaluation

Self-Evaluationでは、まず、自分たちの作ったpresentationの原稿を以下のchecklistを使って確認します。もし、Noになったら、前のunitに戻って改善しましょう。これを行った後は、想定される質問を考え、リハーサルです。

Exercise A

次の（　）内に下の選択肢から適当な文を選びましょう。

Checklist for Presentation Structure

Introduction	
Did I/we offer a proper greeting to the audience?	Yes / No
(a.)	Yes / No
Did I/we explain the structure of our talk? (mapping)	Yes / No
Body	
Did I/we state my/our points clearly?	Yes / No
(b.)	Yes / No
Did I/we provide convincing evidence?	Yes / No
Did I/we repeat or paraphrase the main points?	Yes / No
Did I/we provide clear references?	Yes / No
Conclusion	
(c.)	Yes / No
Did I/we thank the audience and invite them to ask questions?	Yes / No

1. Did I/we use effective signal words/ transitions like “for example?”
2. Did I/we summarize the key point(s)?
3. Did I/we tell the main idea of my/our talk?

■ Checklist が完成したら、自分（たち）の presentation 原稿を再確認してみましょう。

> 原稿が完成したら、もう一度読み直してみましょう。presentation の最後には、audience から質問を受け付けることも大切な presentation の一部です。想定される質問を以下に考えてみましょう。

Exercise B

予想される質問とその答えを英語でそれぞれ 3 つ考えてみましょう。

[Questions]

1. ....

2. ....

3. ....

[Answers]

1. ....

2. ....

3. ....

Exercise C

次の各文がどんな種類の質問にふさわしい返答か考えて、線で結んでみましょう。複数に引かれる場合もあるかも知れません。質問を想定しながら、なぜそうなるか考えてみましょう。

1. To be honest, I think that raises a different issue.
2. That's a very good question.
3. Interesting! What do you think?
4. Well, as I mentioned earlier, ...
5. I'm glad you asked that.
6. I'm afraid I don't have that information with me.
7. I'm afraid I'm not in a position to comment to that.

A. good questions
B. difficult questions
C. unnecessary questions
D. irrelevant questions

いよいよリハーサルです。リハーサルを行うのは、英語の発音やことば使いの確認だけでなく、presentation の内容をしっかり把握しているかどうかを確かめるためです。特に、英文が自分でも覚えられないくらい長く複雑になっていませんか。presenter にとって分かりにくい英語が audience に分かることはありませんね。

Exercise D

次の Evaluation Sheet は、自分（たち）の presentation のリハーサルでも使い、また、他のクラスメイトの presentation を評価する時にも使うものです。評価の観点と内容の意味を確かめながら、適当な語を下の選択肢から入れてみましょう。

Evaluation Sheet

Category	Item	Evaluation
聴衆への配慮 Audience Focus	(a.)	1 poor　2 fair 3 good　4 excellent
	Interaction (Q & A)	1　2　3　4
	Language Choice	1　2　3　4
内容 Contents	Structure and organization	1　2　3　4
	Clear and logical examples	1　2　3　4
身振り・話しぶり Delivery	Good voice and articulation / Smooth delivery	1　2　3　4
	Posture / (b.)	1　2　3　4
表現・ことば使い Language	Transitions / (c.)	1　2　3　4
	(d.)	1　2　3　4
資料 Materials	Contribution to understanding	1　2　3　4
	Slides	1　2　3　4
説得力 Persuasiveness	(e.)	1　2　3　4
	Possibility/Practicality	1　2　3　4
	Benefits for audience	1　2　3　4

1. Evidence　　2. Expression　　3. Eye contact
4. Signal words　　5. Timing and punctuality

Peer Review/Evaluation

Exercise D で完成させた Evaluation Sheet を参考にクラスメイトの presentation を評価してみましょう。評価に使う下の図表は、radar chart といい、数値をイメージ化し、全体のバランスが分かるものです。クラスメイトの presentation を評価することは、自分の presentation の改善にもつながります。Evaluation Sheet に比べて評価の刻み（目盛り）を増やしました。自分（たち）のリハーサルの自己評価と比較してみましょう。また、本番の presentation の後でも反省の意味で、再評価してみましょう。お互いに評価を交換して、改善点を指摘しあうことも、重要です。

Presentation No.: ....

Presenter(s): ....

Theme/ Title: ....

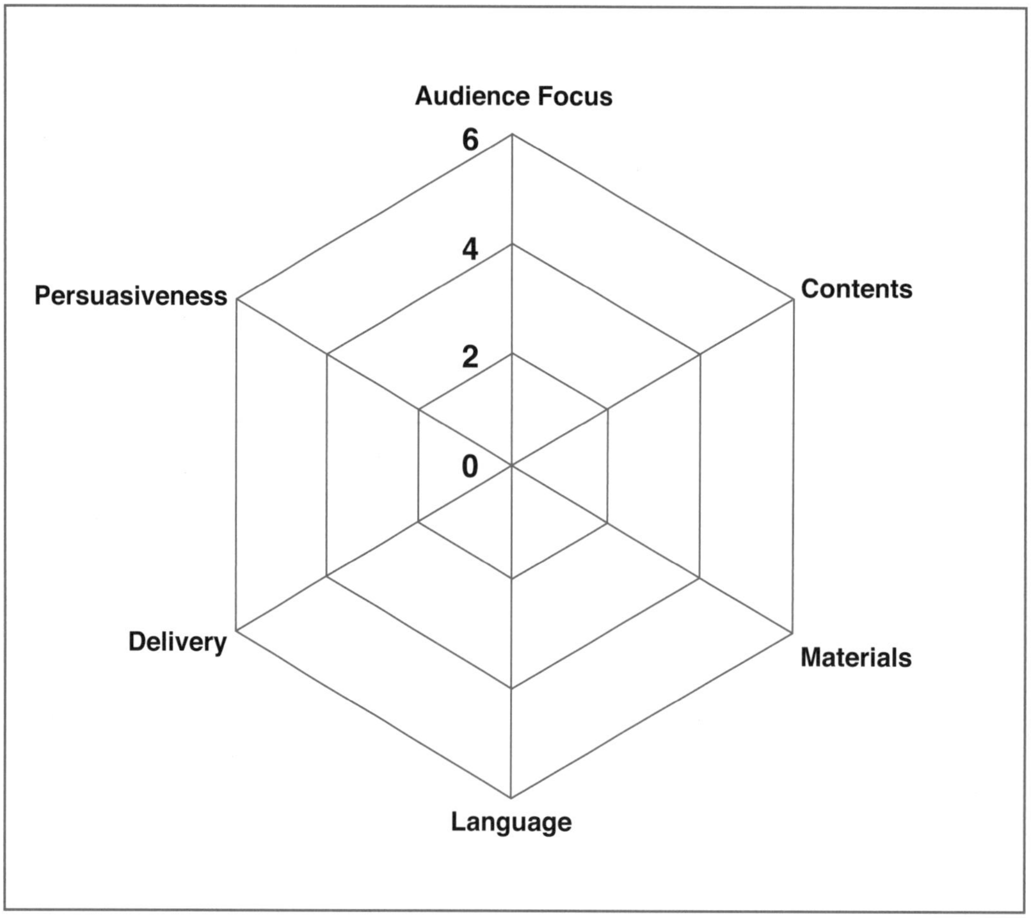

Notes

Appendix

モデルプレゼンテーション原稿

①〜⑨の番号は右ページのスライドが表示されるところです。

① Hello, everyone. I am a student at Nan’un University majoring in linguistics. Thanks for coming here today. ② The objective of today’s presentation is to share with you my ideas about how you can improve your English at university. ③ In this talk, I would like to suggest ways to maintain our motivation to learn English. We all know that entrance exams in Japan are extremely important. Unfortunately, after passing the exams, we often lose motivation to study. Then, what’s a good strategy to keep going? This presentation may offer some ideas. So, let me begin.

④ First of all, try to have fun studying English. Perhaps you enjoy watching American movies or listening to British pop songs. Here is your opportunity to improve your listening skills. ⑤ Another idea is to become friends with someone who is very interested in English. This way, you can help and encourage each other as you struggle to improve your skills. Get to know some foreign students and learn about their culture by communicating in English. It goes without saying that if you have an opportunity to study overseas your English skills will improve dramatically. I understand that many of you are a bit reluctant to leave your friends and family behind. ⑥ So, why not start with a short-term program? How about staying abroad for just a week or two? You will be surprised how much confidence you will gain after just a short stay in an English-speaking country. Most importantly, try to think of how English can be of use to you in the future. Keep in mind, language study does not end with the entrance exams.

⑦ All the ideas I mentioned today are very realistic and in my opinion, effective to give you real-life opportunities to listen to and speak the language. Remember, language study should be a lifelong pursuit. In fact, this is just the beginning of your linguistic journey! Thank you very much for your attention. ⑧ Here are some useful websites. If you would like to know more, don't hesitate to contact me. ⑨ My email is on the last slide. At this point, I am happy to take any questions or comments you may have.

モデルプレゼンテーション使用スライド

①

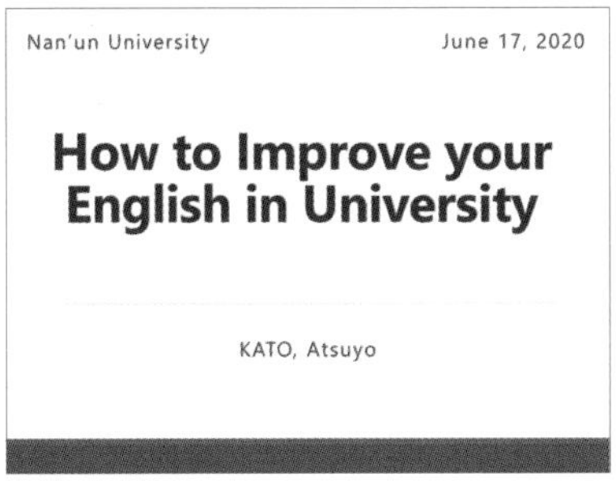

②

③

④

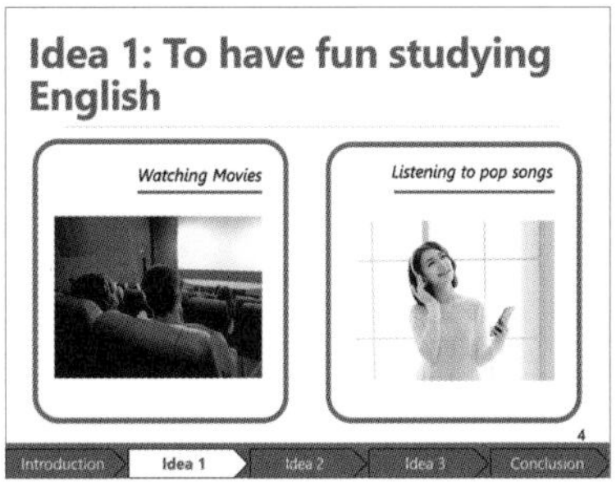

⑤

⑥

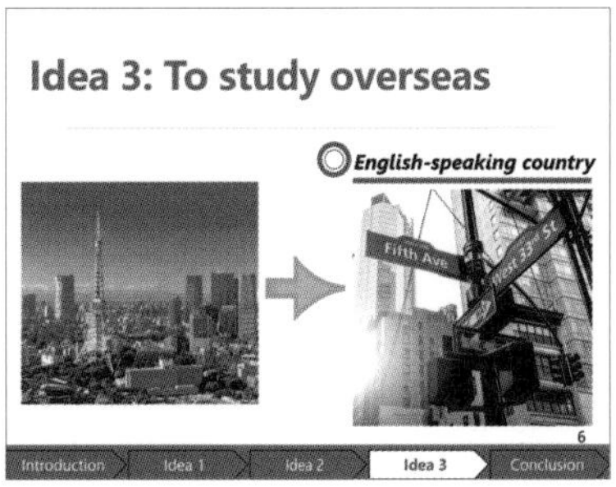

⑦

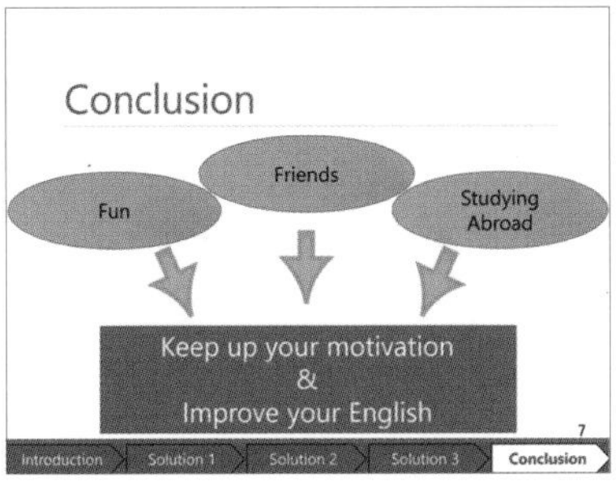

⑧

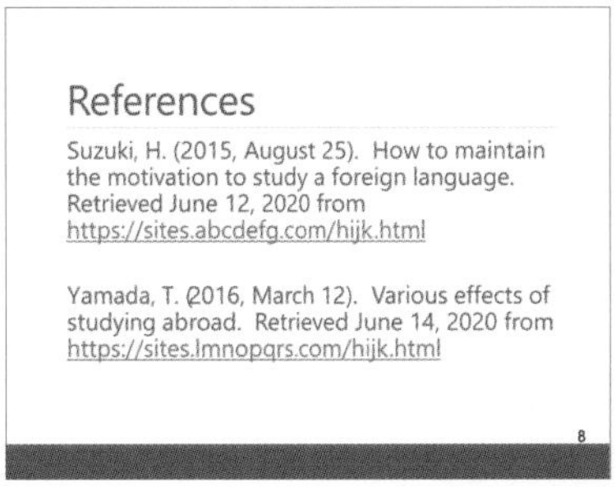

⑨

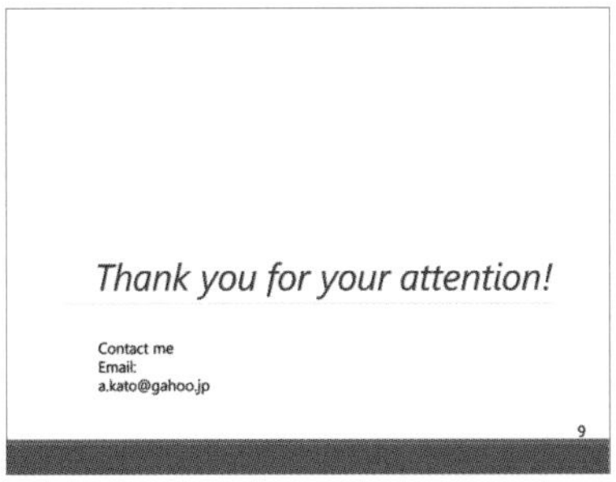

Notes

Message Delivered <Upper Intermediate> [B-903]

パターンで学ぶパラグラフ･ライティングとプレゼンテーション入門〈準上級〉

1　刷　2020年3月26日
2　刷　2022年9月28日

著　者　レオニード・ヨッフェ　Leonid Yoffe
奥　聡一郎　Soichiro Oku
角田　麻里　Mari Kakuta
佐竹　幸信　Yukinobu Satake
森田　彰　Akira Morita

発行者　南雲一範　Kazunori Nagumo
発行所　株式会社　南雲堂
〒162-0801　東京都新宿区山吹町361
NAN'UN-DO Co., Ltd.
361 Yamabuki-cho, Shinjuku-ku, Tokyo 162-0801, Japan
振替口座：00160-0-46863
TEL: 03-3268-2311(営業部：学校関係)
03-3268-2384(営業部：書店関係)
03-3268-2387(編集部)
FAX: 03-3269-2486

編集者　加藤　敦
装　丁　銀月堂
組　版　Office haru
検　印　省　略
コード　ISBN978-4-523-17903-0 C0082

Printed in Japan

E-mail nanundo@post.email.ne.jp
URL https://www.nanun-do.co.jp/